DESIGNING&DOING
SURVEY RESEARCH

SAGE has been part of the global academic community
since 1965, supporting high quality research and learning
that transforms society and our understanding of individuals,
groups and cultures. SAGE is the independent, innovative,
natural home for authors, editors and societies who share
our commitment and passion for the social sciences.

Find out more at: **www.sagepublications.com**

DESIGNING&DOING
SURVEY RESEARCH

LESLEY ANDRES

Los Angeles | London | New Delhi
Singapore | Washington DC

First published 2012

SAGE Publications Ltd
1 Oliver's Yard
55 City Road
London EC1Y 1SP

SAGE Publications Inc.
2455 Teller Road
Thousand Oaks, California 91320

SAGE Publications India Pvt Ltd
B 1/I 1 Mohan Cooperative Industrial Area
Mathura Road
New Delhi 110 044

SAGE Publications Asia-Pacific Pte Ltd
3 Church Street
#10-04 Samsung Hub
Singapore 049483

Library of Congress Control Number: 2011939236

British Library Cataloguing in Publication data

A catalogue record for this book is available from the British Library

ISBN 978-1-84920-812-3
ISBN 978-1-84920-813-0 (Pbk)

Typeset by C&M Digitals (P) Ltd, Chennai, India
Printed and bound by CPI Group (UK) Ltd, Croydon, CR0 4YY
Printed on paper from sustainable resources

MIX
Paper from
responsible sources
FSC
www.fsc.org   FSC® C013604

Table of contents

About the author

Lesley Andres is a Professor in the Department of Educational Studies at the University of British Columbia. Her research and teaching interests include the sociology of education, foundations of higher education, issues of inequality and access, life course research, and quantitative and qualitative research methods.

She is the principal investigator of the Paths on Life's Way Project, a unique Canadian longitudinal study that has combined extensive quantitative and qualitative survey data over a 22 year time frame to examine the lives, actions, and experiences of individuals within a life course framework. Her most recent book, entitled *The Making of a Generation: Children of the 1970s* in Adulthood (co-authored with Johanna Wyn, 2010, University of Toronto Press) is a longitudinal comparative analysis of Canadian and Australian young adults. Also, she is the editor of the Canadian Journal of Higher Education.

In 2010, she was the DAAD (Deutscher Akademischer Austausch Dienst/ German Academic Exchange Service) Chair for International Comparative Studies in Social Sciences at the Bremen International School of Social Sciences, University of Bremen, Germany and Fellow at the Hanse Wissenschaftskolleg (Institute for Advanced Study), Delmenhorst, Germany.

Acknowledgements

The majority of this book was written during my tenure as the DAAD (Deutscher Akademischer Austausch Dienst/German Academic Exchange Service) Chair for International Comparative Studies in Social Sciences at the Bremen International School of Social Sciences (BIGSSS) at the University of Bremen, Germany and as a Fellow at the Hanse Wissenschaftskolleg (Institute for Advanced Study) in Delmenhorst, Germany. I extend warm thanks to Werner Dressel, Susanne Fuchs, Walter and Eva Heinz, Wolfgang Stenzel, and Ansgar Weymann for the support and encouragement they gave me during my stay. In addition, writing retreats at the Weinbau Familie Menhard allowed me to further refine the chapters within the peaceful sanctuary of the Südsteiermark, Austria.

Numerous insightful comments offered over the years by my graduate students in my Survey Research Design course have been incorporated throughout the text. Special thanks are due to my graduate research assistant, Janine Jongbloed, for her skilled assistance and exquisite attention to detail.

In particular, I wish to thank Katie Metzler, Commissioning Editor at Sage, and Anna Horvai, Editorial Assistant, for their unflagging support, advice, assistance, and encouragement. It has been a privilege to work with the entire Sage team.

The Paths on Life's Project, from which many of the examples included in this book have been generated, has received long-term funding from the Social Sciences and Humanities Research Council of Canada. Funding for this project has also been provided by the British Columbia Council on Admissions and Transfer.

Finally, to Hans, *danke*.

ONE

Survey research design – then and now

On almost a daily basis, individuals are confronted with survey research – either as potential participants or as recipients of results. Survey research projects are carried out or commissioned by companies, newspapers, school districts, and other organizations and are administered by individuals, governments, university researchers, polling organizations, and survey research firms. The results of survey research are reported regularly in vehicles such as scholarly research papers or government reports, or in the media ranging from the *New York Times* to *Cosmopolitan* magazine. Today, we read about the results of survey research with the purpose of informing our decisions about a range of activities such as buying a car or adopting a new fitness regime. Conversely, consumers of survey research may have been invited to participate in a survey research project because they had recently purchased a car or engaged in a particular fitness regime. According to Igo (2007: 5), today 'the public is simultaneously object, participant, and audience' of survey research.

In general, there are two major types of survey research. Large-scale surveys such as national censuses, opinion polls, or research projects are carried out by institutions equipped with vast resources in terms of money, staff, and access to databases that are not normally available to an individual researcher. Smaller-scale surveys are carried out by institutions such as schools, post-secondary institutions, hospitals, and other organizations and individuals with the goal of gathering facts about or learning more about the demographic characteristics, behaviours, and attitudes of their students, employees, patients, clients, or members.

These large-scale 'sample' surveys – that is, those based on a representative sample of a larger population – tend to employ standardized questionnaire formats with the goal of generating statistics in order to generalize to a larger population. Such surveys and their related designs are privileged in most survey methods books. Sometimes, other types of survey formats and sampling strategies are not addressed at all. Other times, a sort of schizophrenic approach is employed in survey methods books in that the topics of interviewing, non-probabilistic sampling, and open-ended questions are introduced or touched upon, but are not fully developed to the same extent as studies that are based on probabilistic designs (those employing random samples). For example, authors of many survey texts consider the group administration of a survey, for example within a classroom setting, as legitimate. However, the same authors either do not include or are critical of the convenience sample (again, students conveniently located within a classroom) as a legitimate sampling strategy. As such, these alternative approaches are usually relegated to an 'inferior' status or condemned – what Weisberg (2005: 237) calls 'usual textbook injunctions against [non-probability sampling]'. Examples of survey research in many existing texts are based on large probability samples that are (1) not feasible for the small-scale researcher to carry out, and (2) not particularly instructive when trying to learn how to conduct survey research. The word 'interview' in many textbooks means highly structured interviews and does not embrace the full range of uses of interviews in survey methods.

Few researchers have the privilege, ability, or desire to collect data through some form of probability sample. Access to lists of potential respondents is often restricted; only large data collection centres have the resources and political clout to gain access to such lists and carry out large-scale projects. Although the survey instrument and sample are integral and interrelated dimensions of survey research, the former does not need to be limited exclusively to a set of standardized questions presented to a sample with the intention of generalizing to larger populations. Within both of these dimensions there are many options.

In reality, most real-world survey research is conducted on a much smaller scale, to specifically targeted audiences. This book is designed to help those – for example, senior undergraduate and graduate students, small business owners, institutional researchers – to design meaningful surveys through the skilful crafting of questions that are posed to the audience or audiences best suited to answering the questions.

Many texts on survey research design are grounded solidly in the positivistic paradigm and related notions of objectivity and parsimony. However, because the social science world that we investigate is full of subjectivities and objectivities, survey research need not be limited to a tight set of rules that limit our ability to capture life as experienced by our respondents. The phrase 'survey research' provides a rubric for many types of approaches, ranging from self-administered to interviewer-administered approaches. Because we can maintain rigour through strong design, data collection from different perspectives should be encouraged.

In addition, survey research can be carried out in a myriad of ways to ask questions ranging from open-ended interviews to those that are closed-ended and strictly standardized. Many types of approaches, ranging from pen-and-paper mail-out surveys to face-to-face interviews conducted via webcam can be employed. Surveys can be free-standing or can be embedded in larger research designs such as ethnographies, case studies, or experimental research.

Questionnaires, face-to-face interviews, and focus groups all belong to the rubric of survey research. In addition, either probabilistic (based on random samples), non-probabilistic techniques (purposive or not based on random samples), or combinations of both types of sampling designs can be employed. Statistics can be generated from surveys, text can be analysed qualitatively from interviews or open-ended survey questions, or these methods can be combined by, for example, quantifying interview data by reading codes and data stored in qualitative software programs into statistical software programs. The goal of survey research may be to generalize to larger populations *or* it may be intended to be *transferable* – that is, the 'findings will be useful to others in similar situations, with similar research questions or questions of practice' (Marshall and Rossman, 2006: 201). In other words, survey research can and should be conducted from both quantitative *and* qualitative perspectives.

This is not a new idea. In the past many approaches to data collection were included under the label 'survey research'. The 'paradigm wars' that were prominent at the end of the twentieth century have not been resolved but rather have 'agreed to a détente' (Bergman, 2008b: 2). In terms of survey research, the quantitative–qualitative divide remains in that quantitative researchers continue to resist the idea that open-ended interviewing is a valid form of survey research (see Fowler, 2009) and qualitative researchers are surprised to learn that when they interview people to make statements that extend beyond the sample, they are actually conducting survey research! In many instances, by informing themselves of some of the key tenets of survey research design, qualitative researchers could strengthen their research projects which would, in turn, be more rigorous and hence more credible, and quantitative researchers could expand the results of their findings by enlivening them with the voices of respondents. In 1944, Paul Lazarsfeld, a leading figure in twentieth-century American sociology and survey research, addressed what he described as 'two philosophies of research … one wedded to so-called in-depth interviewing, and the other content with more objective methods of research' (Lazarsfeld, 1944) and concluded that a combination of methods (p. 60) would result in improving research design, analysis, and interpretation. In his 1962 presidential address to the American Sociological Association, Lazarsfeld said that early in his academic career he was assigned the task of analysing the occupational choices of young people. While it was relatively straightforward to conduct analyses to portray relationships among choices, social stratification, and age differences, problems arose in trying to interpret the reasons for choices. He noted that 'reasons' provided were contradictory and led to ambiguous responses that defied meaningful analysis. He concluded that 'an investigator's lack of skill in the art of asking "why" questions led to meaningless statistical results' (1962: 758). 'Ever since', he asserted, 'I have continued to search for sound ways for making empirical studies of action' (p. 758).

Surveys that are more quantitatively oriented will include more closed-ended questions, and those that are more qualitatively oriented will include more open-ended questions. However, considerable advances in *mixed methods research* design invite us to consider including both types of question and to use different types of survey format, such as mail-out questionnaires and interviews. In fact, the variety of data collection formats and ways of posing questions to respondents makes survey research a naturally occurring mixed methods design. Survey research, in and of itself, is a large, heterogeneous family of methods which do not fit tidily into either a quantitative or qualitative box.

TEXT BOX 1.1

The movie *Kitchen Stories,* directed by Bent Hamer, provides a delightful example of research paradigm wars.

http://en.wikipedia.org/wiki/Kitchen_Stories

Trying to separate the two approaches and to downplay or dismiss the latter does indeed hamper (Bergman, 2008c) the creative ways that survey research alone, or in combination with other types of research, can produce rich findings. Often, the choice of survey method is based on the researcher's training, too often in one or other of the methodological camps. As a result, studies are designed not according to the research questions at hand, but rather to conform to the researcher's analytical skill set(s). As we shall see in Chapter 9, advances in analytical software programs have broken down the barriers between quantitative and qualitative analysis, rendering combinations of the various data collection methods no longer problematic. As such, 'specific data collection and analysis [may] now be connected far more directly and explicitly to a research focus, research context, and research design' (Bergman, 2008c: 18).

Historically, survey research embraced a wide variety of data collection methods. In the next section, I provide a brief overview of the history of survey research.

A short history of survey research

Gathering data on individuals has a long history, with various censuses dating back to antiquity. The first documented census occurred in China more than

4000 years ago (http://www.thecanadianencyclopedia.com/index.cfm?PgNm=
TCE&Params=A1ARTA0020060). Several references to census-taking in relation
to taxation occur in the Christian Bible. Originally, data on individuals were
collected primarily for reasons of taxation and military service. The Domesday
Book of 1086, commissioned by William the Conqueror, documented the land
holdings and livestock of most of the English population for the purpose of levy-
ing taxes. The male census in Norway in the 1660s was conducted for a similar
purpose. The oldest documented complete nominal census – that is, containing
the names of the members of the population – was in Iceland in 1703, where the
following data were collected: name, age, and position in the household, along
with health information and whether the person was a pauper without abode
(Garðarsdóttir and Guðmundsson, 2005; Tomasson, 1977).

TEXT BOX 1.2

A description of world censuses can be found in Wikipedia:

http://en.wikipedia.org/wiki/Censusnsus

Sweden stakes claim to the first comprehensive endeavour in population statistics, the *Tablellverket* in 1749 (Sköld, 2004). Today, Sweden remains a leader in gathering data on its population. Eventually censuses became more all-encompassing
by first linking commercialism with economic growth and then extending to the
physical and moral health of the population (Thorvaldson, 2007).

Nominal censuses began in Great Britain in 1801, Denmark in 1834, Sweden
in 1860, and Norway in 1865. The first national census was undertaken in the
USA in 1790, Canada in 1871, and Australia in 1881. Simultaneously, other
non-state organizations in Britain, Germany, France, the USA and elsewhere
began collecting 'vital statistics' data for purposes such as monitoring disease
and creating insurance tables. As Igo (2007: 7) points out, 'Western countries
in the nineteenth century witnessed a wave of surveying by private citizens
and philanthropists, producing a veritable "avalanche of numbers" in the
service of industrial and social reform'. In addition, there is evidence that in
the 1800s surveys were being conducted within academic circles. For example, Max Weber, a sociologist and political scientist most famous for his work
The Protestant Ethic and the Spirit of Capitalism, took part in six data collection
endeavours involving the administration of questionnaires to individuals. The
first, carried out in 1890, included the study of workers' attitudes (Lazarsfeld
and Oberschall, 1965).

However, the notion of *survey* in these early studies meant something quite
different to what it does today. This is best exemplified by the research of Charles

Booth at the end of the nineteenth and beginning of the twentieth century in London. Booth has been called the 'founding father'[1] (Converse, 1987: 1) of the empirical tradition in the social sciences, and it is worth taking a few minutes to examine his accomplishments.

Shortly after moving to London in 1875, the shipping magnate Charles Booth became passionately interested in the problems of poverty and unemployment plaguing the city that 'politically and administratively ... had scarcely advanced beyond the Middle Ages' (Fried and Elman, 1968: xv). He engaged in debates and discussions with politicians, socialists, and social workers who were unable to adequately answer his key concern: 'exactly how the poor lived, exactly how discontented they were, how concretely they might be helped' (Fried and Elman, 1968: xvi). By creatively piecing together available information such as census data and drawing on a plurality of data gathering approaches, Booth set out to answer this question and focused his attention initially on the East End of London.

TEXT BOX 1.3

Charles Booth 1902.

Visit the Charles Booth Online Archives at the London School of Economics: http://booth.lse.ac.uk/
Courtesy of Senate House Library, University of London, Goldsmiths Library, MS797/11/96/2.

---

[1]Lazarsfeld (1961) points out that this distinction more accurately belongs to Frederic LePlay for his empirical work on European families.

He collaborated with London School Board visitors who were able to provide detailed accounts of all families with children of preschool age. In order to gather information about the poor who did not have children, Booth extended his data collection endeavours to include sources such as Poor Law statistics, registered lodging houses documented in police reports (Fried and Elman, 1968: xviii), and what we might today call 'focus groups' with colleagues of diverse political persuasions (Englander and O'Day, 1995). Through a detailed analysis of the data, Booth and his small team of colleagues and staff constructed an eight-category economic classification system and eventually created a definition of the 'poverty line'. Booth and his team set out to conduct a massive endeavour interviewing members of households and lodging residences. The collected data were used to create colour-coded poverty maps corresponding to his economic levels.

In the resulting four volumes comprising the *Poverty Series*, Booth concluded that one in three East Londoners lived in abject poverty, well in excess of the figure of one in four reported a few years earlier in the *Pall Mall Gazette*, which, at the time, he thought was grossly exaggerated. Over the next several years, his investigations extended to the study of industry (the five-volume *Industry Series*) and religion (the seven-volume *Religious Series*). Together with a final summary volume, a total of 17 volumes had been produced. In addition, his observations on the relationship between old age and poverty eventually led to the passing of the 1908 Old Age Pensions Act in Britain (Fried and Elman, 1968: xxxiii–xxxiv).

Booth's ability to carry out such a monumental study can be summarized by his statement in the final volume: 'The root idea with which I began … was that every fact I needed to know was known to someone and that the information had simply to be collected and put together' (quoted in Pfautz, 1967). Without tools such as computers and related statistical and qualitative data analysis programs, Booth employed multiple methods of data collection – a mixed methods design employing methodological *triangulation* in today's language – including analyses of existing census data, qualitative topographical descriptions, detailed qualitative descriptions of the people's behaviours, and their habits within the societal contexts in which they were affected. Booth even had first-hand experience of the living conditions of poor families by occasionally renting a room in their homes.

He also grappled with common methodological dilemmas of interviewee bias and non-compliance, and challenges in data comparability which he sought to remedy through large-scale data collection and the construction of structured interview schedules and reports (Englander and O'Day, 1995: 34). His work has been credited with leading to the development of modern-day sampling methods (Lazarsfeld, 1962: 761). However, over the course of the twentieth century, instead of embracing complexity, survey research as envisioned and enacted by Booth narrowed dramatically in scope.

After having received favourable reviews in American media and scholarly journals, Booth's work served as a model for many American studies of communities, including examinations of the slums of Chicago and the black population in Philadelphia. Those engaged in such research embraced the 'social survey in the style of Booth' and employed 'omnivorous' approaches (Converse, 1987: 3) to data collection in order to produce detailed vivid descriptions of the lives and living conditions of their study populations. Often the research was undertaken by social movement groups and 'amateur' social surveyors who wanted not only to describe but also to improve social conditions, and funded by philanthropists and municipal governments. Eventually, however, such research would become located in the more professional settings of the university and government agencies and would move toward disinterested 'objective' research and away from research with the goal of enacting social change (Igo, 2007).

According to Igo (2007), '"scientific" surveyors elevated scholarly neutrality as a badge of honor, marginalizing the kind of knowledge that could be gained through "value-laden" social activism' (p. 28) and 'what united the diverse practices given the imprimateur "social science" was not a resolve to alleviate social problems but an embrace of certain techniques: objective observation, intense fact-collecting, and quantification. This perspective on social life, and the kind of knowledge that flowed from it, were considered uniquely modern scientific achievements' (p. 28).

Curiously, the first social science study to gain best-selling status did so based on an 'objective' scientific approach that was based on 'facts'. The study *Middletown* which documented an apparently 'typical' American city, was conducted by Robert and Helen Lynd (1929) who made it even more typical by excluding the black and immigrant population and the influence of the Ku Klux Klan from their research. According to Igo (2007: 74–75), 'the technical apparatus of social science and its particular style of reportage ... could trump the conditions of its creation'. This study marked the beginning of the shift to the protean (Converse, 1987) social survey. However, this approach seems more procrustean in nature, where the multi-methodological limbs of survey research design were severed and only the emaciated torso of 'objective scientific facts' remained. Employment of '"the" scientific method' to gather only 'the facts', 'rather than ... slippery opinions' (Converse, 1987: 31), became the goals of the social surveyor. Well into the 1940s 'the "survey" was still a number of things – almost anything empirical' (p. 39), including contextual descriptions of communities, individual and aggregate data collected in the field, and detailed data collected on individuals through, for example, school records. Steadily, the focus of survey research shifted to that of the individual record, the standardization of questionnaire wording, probability theory based on random samples, which led to the use of the term 'sample survey' (Converse, 1987). By the end of the twentieth century, 'social scientific methods, findings, and vocabularies were omnipresent. What had been quite unfamiliar several generations earlier had become as natural – and invisible – as the air the Americans breathed' (Igo, 2007: 13).

Definition of survey research

Over the course of the last century, the definition and related practice of survey research has moved away from the idea of conducting a broad *overview* or a 'comprehensive vision of the whole' (Converse, 1987: 19) while simultaneously *overseeing* in the sense of 'examining in detail, scrutinizing close up, inspecting' by employing 'a mélange of techniques – the more the better' (p. 18) to collect data. Data employed in such studies ranged from existing aggregate population data to detailed household budgets which documented the amount of meat consumed by a family in a given week. Eventually the definition of a social survey was narrowed, but it still encompassed the following: (1) data collected in the field, as opposed to in a laboratory setting; (2) organization of the data by the individual record but still employing a multitude of methods to gather data on the individual; and (3) a means to establish the value or extent of the phenomena under investigation, by either counting or measuring some or all of the information gathered. Also, 'a patchwork of different kinds of data, collected by different means and processed in different ways', was employed (Converse, 1987: 33).

Eventually, survey research morphed into the *sample survey* and related notions of 'scientific', 'objective', and 'standardized' gathering of the 'facts' through 'probability sampling'. The term *survey method* began to be used 'to refer rather grandly to the surveyors' use of *"the" scientific method* as they gathered "the facts". The context here was that of a science as a form of knowledge, constructed of hard, objective measurements rather than slippery opinions, private emotions or intuitions, or exaggerated political hopes' (Converse, 1987: 32), with an increasing focus on measurement. Yet, the 'facts' gathered in survey research are what Cantril (1951: x) suggests most often refer to 'an individual's assumptive world' – a world constructed and reported by an individual in a way that allows one to characterize oneself as a human being. As Sudman and Bradburn (1982) point out, whereas some 'facts' about an individual – for example birth date or occupation – in principle are verifiable, the ethical, practical, and often the only way of gathering most information on behaviour, attitudes, beliefs, and opinions most efficiently is through asking individuals through survey research. As such, individuals' responses are for the most part unverifiable.

Today, it is not uncommon to find the following definitions of survey research:

The purpose of the survey is to produce statistics – that is quantitative or numerical descriptions of some aspects of the study population. (Fowler, 2009)

Sample surveys are typically conducted to estimate the distribution of characteristics in a population. (Dillman, 2000: 9)

At the root of sample survey research is the discipline of statistics .... The ultimate goal of sample survey research is to allow researchers to generalize about a large population by studying only a small portion of that population. (Rea and Parker, 2005: xii, 4)

Although all of these definitions are correct, they only pertain to one type of survey research – the *sample* survey. Often, *sample* survey research is precisely the most appropriate approach to a given project. However, not all surveys require that a smaller sample of the population be drawn. Sometimes, the entire population is easily accessible, eliminating several sources of error. Sometimes, the target population is elusive and other sampling methods (e.g., snowball sampling) must be employed. Sometimes, there is no intention to generalize the findings (e.g., in an in-house research project designed to improve a company's competitive advantage). Sometimes, the goal is not generalizability, but to invite readers to determine whether the findings of a particular study conducted with a specific group of people in a particular context can be transferable to other settings. In other words, survey research is not limited to a probability sample onto which questions are superimposed.

Moreover, while most survey research produces statistics with the goal of 'convert[ing] people into questionnaires and finally into cross-tabulations' (Lazarsfeld, 1962: 759), the words of respondents can also be employed to assess the value of a given phenomenon and, if it is desirable to do so, can indeed be quantified by counting their frequency of occurrence. At minimum, more qualitative questions incorporated into survey research can be used for various purposes, including pretesting new ideas by checking assumptions behind and refining these ideas (Lazarsfeld, 1962: 767), clarifying respondents' answers to a question, or helping to clarify or interpret a statistical relationship (Lazarsfeld, 1944). Survey data collected qualitatively can be free-standing in analyses or combined with quantitative findings.

The goal of this book is to put all of the dimensions that belong under the rubric of survey research on an equal playing field, so that the focus becomes one of asking questions of the right people to elicit meaningful answers that will advance our understanding of a given topic with the goal of improving practice, policy, research, and theory. This book draws particularly on the wisdom of Charles Booth, Paul Lazarsfeld, Stanley Payne, Seymour Sudman, and Norman Bradburn who understood that survey research is as much an art as it is a science. In other words, the purpose of this text is to return to the art of asking questions, or, to use Bingham and Moore's (1959) definition, to start from the vantage point of having a 'conversation directed to a definite purpose' from which the other components of survey research – including sampling, modes of administration – follow. I do, however, agree that in the early twentieth century, 'the word *survey* [was] sometimes used so vaguely and broadly to cover almost the whole empirical waterfront of social science, and it is confusing to stretch the definition so far' (Converse, 1987: 20). This book will be limited to survey research that engages in asking questions of individuals with the intention of extending the results beyond the individual study respondents. Also, I will emphasize the necessity of a systematic approach to survey research design – however, this must be appropriate to the purpose, research questions, and conceptual framework(s) of the study. Survey research is in harmony with mixed methods approaches as promoted by mixed methods researchers (Bergman, 2008a; Cresswell et al., 2008; de Leeuw and Hox, 2008; Plano Clark and Cresswell, 2008; Plowright, 2011; Tashakkori and Teddlie, 2008, 2010).

I do not start out from the vantage point of objectivity. I agree with Cantril that the notion of the 'objective scientist' is a myth. As he asserts, 'real scientific research of any kind is rooted in value judgments' (1951: x), beginning with the formulation of the problem through to implications of the finding and recommendations for policy, practice, theory, and further research. The art of survey research is the ability to shape value judgements into a meaningful and powerful survey research design. According to Daston and Galison (2007: 16), historically the quest for scientific objectivity 'was about that new form of unprejudiced, unthinking, blind sight'.

And I concur with Stanley Payne that a good survey researcher needs to be a jack- or jill-of-all-trades, and not simply a statistician, to be able to follow through with all of the tasks involved in survey research as specified in each of the chapters in this book and beyond. Rather than starting from the premise that the purpose of survey research is to produce statistics and then to contort the design to produce 'objective' and parsimonious results, I side with Payne (1951: 6) in that there is no 'magic way of reducing a complex matter of people's attitudes, wishes, aspirations to some simple wording which will not bias the returns', with Katz (1946) in that good survey design 'must approach the problem from many angles, ask the dependent questions, explore the reasons why, seek the relevant background material and personal data', and with Lazarsfeld (1962: 767) in that new generations of social science researchers should have the courage to embrace complexity by the 'interweaving of quantitative and qualitative technique, of simultaneous research on individual and organizational levels'. As Bergman (2008b: 2) points out, many researchers – myself included – have avoided or disregarded the constraints of the methods camps and have been employing mixed methods designs throughout the last century, suggesting that 'apparently mixed methods research works far better in practice than in theory'.

Survey research and ethics

As with all research, survey researchers must ensure that they follow the tenets of ethical conduct in each phase of a survey research study. Survey research belongs to the category of behavioural research and hence is guided by the policies, guidelines, and practices of behavioural ethical review boards.

Also, research granting agencies provide extensive guidelines and specify requirements regarding the ethical conduct of research which are implemented through institutional ethical review boards at, for example, post-secondary or medical institutions. Other institutions such as schools or indigenous communities may have their own ethics protocols.

Respect for human dignity is central to the ethical conduct of research. Respect for human dignity revolves around the following core principles: 'respect for persons, concern for welfare, and justice' (Canadian Institutes of Health Research et al., 2010: 8). Because survey research design is multifaceted, the implications in terms of ethics are complex. Rather than devoting a single section or chapter to ethics, throughout each of the chapters of this book I have addressed the topic of ethics as it arises. A text box with the heading **Ethics Alert!** such as the one below will signal to the reader that ethical issues are at hand.

TEXT BOX 1.4

Ethics Alert!

Watch for this alert throughout the book.

TEXT BOX 1.5

Ethics Alert!

Ethical guidelines are specified by professional associations such as the following:

Social Research Association in the UK http://www.the-sra.org.uk/documents/pdfs/ethics03.pdf

Australian Psychological Society http://www.psychology.org.au/about/ethics/

Canadian Sociological Association http://www.csa-scs.ca/code-of-ethics

American Sociological Association http://www.asanet.org/about/ethics.cfm

---

Summary

The purpose of this chapter was to provide an overview of survey research design, to present a brief history of survey research, and to specify a definition of survey research from which subsequent chapters will unfold. Finally, an introduction to the topic of ethics was provided. In the next chapter, I map out the process of survey research design, beginning with the identification of the research problem and related questions through to preparation for analysis. In each of the remaining chapters, each facet, as presented in Chapter 2, will be explicated further.

Exercises

1 Describe your research problem in general terms. The problem should focus on a specific issue that interests you.

2 Using the information presented in this chapter, can survey research be employed to address your research problem? If so, why? If not, why not?

3 Consider whether your research problem can be best addressed through a self-administered survey (e.g., pen-and-paper survey or web-based survey) or an interview-administered survey (e.g., telephone survey or face-to-face interview).

4 Envision whether a mixed methods design could be employed to enhance the richness of the research findings.

Further reading

Booth, C. (1891). *Labour and Life of the People in London*. London: Macmillan.

Converse, J. M. (1987). *Survey Research in the United States. Roots and Emergence 1890–1960*. Berkeley: University of California Press.

Denzin, N. K. (1989). *The Research Act. A Theoretical Introduction to Sociological Methods*. Englewood Cliffs, NJ: Prentice Hall.

Igo, S. E. (2007). *The Averaged American: Surveys, Citizens, and the making of a Mass Public*. Cambridge, MA: Harvard University Press.

TWO

Mapping out the survey research process

Designing a survey research project is not a linear process. Rather, it involves a mosaic of tasks and related decisions that are initially often very disparate but eventually come together to form a coherent approach to the survey research process. The survey researcher must truly be a jack- or jill-of-all-trades, as Stanley Payne (1951) pointed out long ago. Good survey design requires that the researcher possess the following: theoretical expertise; a good grasp of sampling theory; professional ethical and political astuteness; the ability to wordsmith compelling and clear questions; a flare for graphic design in terms of survey lay-out; technical expertise to construct an appealing study including, if appropriate, web-based surveys; shrewdness in crafting a sound budget and realistic schedule; and the skill to conduct statistical and/or qualitative analyses of the data and prepare documents for publication. Each facet in the mosaic of decisions must be carefully predetermined as a decision at one point in the process is likely to affect other decisions.

The purpose of this chapter is to provide an overview of the components of survey research design. The entire research design process is laid out in summary format with the goal of sensitizing the reader to the key issues involved in the survey research endeavour. I avoid using the terms 'steps' or 'sequence of events' because this process is iterative. Instead, I use the term 'facet' in the sense of the many surfaces involved in the survey research design process. Each facet of the process is highlighted in Figure 2.1, adapted from Blaxter et al.'s (2010) research spiral. Throughout Chapters 3–10, I will continue to elaborate on each of these components.

Identifying the research problem and related questions

Ideas for survey research projects can emerge from many sources. University students may be motivated to pursue a certain topic based on course work

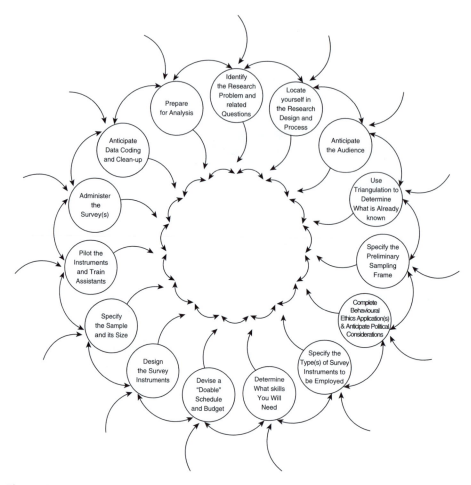

Figure 2.1 Facets of the survey research process

Source: Blaxter, L., Hughes, C., and Tight, M. (2010). *How to Research*. Buckingham: Open University Press. Reproduced in modified form with the kind permission of Open University Press. All rights reserved.

undertaken in their undergraduate or graduate studies. Gaps in the research literature or the availability of research funding for certain topics often provide opportunities for further exploration. Alternatively, ideas can emerge from real-life situations in the work place, or from involvement in organizations such as sporting clubs, voluntary or professional associations, or non-profit organizations. Regardless of the source of the idea, as a prospective survey researcher the first question you must ask yourself is: *Is survey methodology the right method for the topic at hand?*

Cartoon 2.1

Survey research is multifaceted and versatile in that differing degrees of breadth and depth of a research topic can be explored, depending on the approach or combination of approaches taken (e.g., mail-out surveys versus face-to-face interviews, or both) and the degree of structure associated with each approach (e.g., closed-ended versus open-ended questions). However, survey research is usually limited to questions of description, behaviour, attitudes, and opinions and is intended to generalize or be transferred in some way beyond the original sample. Survey research is not appropriate for research interested in human interaction; ethnographic research approaches are much better suited to such questions. Also, survey research is typically not able to capture directly the effects of a 'treatment' such as exposure to different styles of teaching or the effects of a drug on the treatment of a disease – here, experimental design would be appropriate. However, survey research is often employed as a supplementary form of data gathering. For example, in an ethnographic study of a large corporation, pen-and-paper surveys may be carried out to assess the attitudes and opinions (e.g., levels of satisfaction) of employees. Clinical trials of new drugs may be supplemented with questionnaires to determine the side effects experienced by study participants.

Typical research questions conducive to survey research are as follows: What factors influence how parents choose schools for their children? What are adolescents' behaviours and attitudes regarding drinking and driving? What are university students' attitudes toward income-contingent student loan repayment plans? Such questions invite investigations about description (e.g., age, gender, income, educational level, family composition), behaviour (e.g., drinking), attitudes and opinions (e.g., views about what constitutes a good school). Combinations of the above, such as attitudes by age group and gender, serve to strengthen a survey research design.

Locating yourself in the research design and process

The notion of the 'objective researcher' is a long-standing myth (Onwuegbuzie, 2002). Like any other type of researcher, you as a survey researcher (perhaps together with a team, a stakeholder group, or a client) define the research problem and make decisions about every dimension of the survey research project specified in Figure 2.1. As such, decisions are based on your subjectivities, assumptions, and values. Decisions that are within the purview of the researcher to create boundaries around the research (e.g., location of the study, the nature of study participants) are called *delimitations* of a study. Boundaries that are external to the researcher (e.g., inability to gain access to certain populations), are called *limitations* of a study. As Cantril (1951: vii) pointed out long ago,

> those of us engaged in 'research' like to think of ourselves as 'scientists'. We like to think that there are certain 'rules' which we can discover and follow in order to be 'objective'. And we tend to think that if we can only quantify our material and manipulate it statistically, then, and only then, are we being 'scientific'. Hence, much of our research deals with technical problems of measurement.

Instead, he argues that outstanding survey researchers are 'great artists in the sense that they had the intuitive capacity to ask themselves the right questions at the right time' (p. viii).

Contrary to viewing ourselves as 'potential contaminant[s], something to be separated out, neutralized, minimized, standardized and controlled' (Fine et al., 2000: 109), today it is recommended that, as the researcher, you make yourself transparent by locating yourself in the research. This *positionality* usually involves identifying your many selves that are relevant to the research on dimensions such as gender, sexual orientation, race/ethnicity, educational attainment, occupation, parental status, and work and life experience. Merriam et al. (2001: 411) state that 'positionality is determined by where one stands in relation to the "other"'. Several useful concepts can be used to help orient oneself in relation to one's research project. These include *insider/outsider* and *indigenous* or *external status* and the related idea of *hybridity*.

The notion of *insider/outsider status* is not an either/or viewpoint. Rather, the degree to which one is an insider or outsider and its related advantages and disadvantages can shift depending on the stage of the research and the nature of interactions at any given point in time. By virtue of having the power and authority to conduct a research project, you as apparent insider may find yourself as an outsider in your own culture (Fine et al., 2000; Merriam et al., 2001). Another dimension worth considering in relation to the insider/outsider notion is the extent to which one is *indigenous* or *external* to a culture (Banks, 1998). The concept of *hybridity* simultaneously extends and blurs the insider/outsider notion *vis-à-vis* the indigenous/external concept in that researchers are 'minimally bicultural in terms of belonging simultaneously to the world of engaged scholarship and the world of everyday life' (Narayan, 1993: 672).

Such simple positionality is, however, only a beginning step toward locating yourself in a survey research project. It is also critical to think about power relationships and dynamics between you as a researcher and the researched, and the extent to which the researched can and should be empowered as part of the research process.

TEXT BOX 2.1

Ethics Alert!

Be aware that power dynamics between the researcher and the researched is an ethical concern.

Also, such reflexivity allows you to identify any conflicts of interest. Ethical considerations of informed consent and assent help to address issues of power. Fine et al. (2000: 108) stress the importance of 'think[ing] through the power, obligations, and responsibilities of social research'.

Anticipating the audience

The flip side of locating yourself in the research is to anticipate the audience(s) of your research. The audience(s) can be any or all of the following: an academic research committee, the academic community, a client who commissions the research, an employer, or the general public. Familiarity with what is expected by a given audience in advance of undertaking a survey research project will assist in addressing each step in Figure 2.1 and tailoring the final document accordingly.

Audiences may be deliberate and targeted, or they may be unintended. Fine et al. (2000) warn that while research can be used to enlighten various audiences with the intention of improving the well-being of our research participants, findings can also be distorted and misread by, for example, policy-makers with certain agendas. It is with these concerns in mind that survey researchers choose questions, recruit research participants, report findings, and draw conclusions and recommendations for policy and practice.

Using triangulation to determine
what is already known

Of all the facets involved in the research process, determining what is already known is arguably one of the most important. Good detective work at this stage will lead to a stronger, more relevant, and more timely research project. One way to tackle this sometimes overwhelming facet is to employ triangulation. Simply, triangulation requires the employment of multiple sources, including theory, methods, data collection strategies, or analytical techniques with the purpose of interrogating each type of resource.

TEXT BOX 2.2

International comparative research

Adding international comparative research to your review of the literature may enhance the richness of your research project.

At each level of investigation of what is already known, triangulation can be employed. Once an initial topic or research question has been identified, you should begin by reading widely and across disciplinary boundaries. For example, if you are interested in the relationship between educational attainment and happiness, you will read in the areas of education, psychology, sociology, political science, and economics. Such breadth will then lead to an understanding of the range of theoretical, methodological, and analytical perspectives used to investigate this topic. International comparative perspectives should be considered to determine how different jurisdictions frame research on a given topic and to decide whether a multiple-site study would be appropriate or feasible in your research.

Triangulation should be used for three purposes: *convergence, inconsistency*, and *contradiction* (Mathison, 1988). In other words, triangulation helps to 'trouble' existing literature and research by determining similarities (convergence), inconsistent and/or ambiguous claims, propositions, or results (inconsistency), and disparate approaches, theories, perspectives, analytical techniques, and results (contradiction). The result is informational pluralism.

Through triangulation, a thorough examination of the literature will be carried out, and further reading will be identified in the reference lists of existing literature. Conclusions and recommendations for further research will help

---

you further refine your research questions. Also, the availability of existing databases should be determined. Perhaps you may conclude that the use of an existing database (called secondary data analysis) can be employed to address your research adequately and more cost efficiently. For example, the World Values Survey enterprise collects data on 97 societies. Alternatively, using data from an existing database and adding on a smaller component of primary data collection in the form of a questionnaire or interviews may result in a strong research design.

Through triangulation, survey instruments in existing studies can be examined, compared, and scrutinized for their usefulness in your work. Survey instruments from national databases such as the census or general social surveys, UNESCO databases, and country-specific databases such as the British Cohort Study or the German Socio-Economic Panel Study can be examined. Many of these databases allow free access to the data. Canada is an exception in this regard as most of the data collected by Statistics Canada require that users must apply formally for permission to use a given data set.

Once permission is granted, the data can be accessed only at a research data centre. Researchers wishing to use such data must determine whether the constraints of being required to conduct research within the confines of a research data centre are outweighed by the strength of the data set.

TEXT BOX 2.3

Consider examining survey instruments from other countries as a source of inspiration and information for your survey research project.

During this facet of the survey research process, the research librarian is an invaluable resource. S/he will possess up-to-date skills with existing and ever-changing research tools such as search engines.

Another way of determining what is already known may be to talk with key informants. Such informants may be colleagues in the case of a work-based study, government officials, experts in a given field, or individuals similar to the sample you intend to study. Information from these individuals and groups can be collected informally through conversations, or more formally in the form of fact-finding interviews or focus groups.

At this point, the research problem and related questions identified in the first facet of this exercise should be revisited, reworked, and refined. A more detailed discussion about this facet is taken up in Chapter 3.

Specifying the preliminary sampling frame

Specifying the research sample(s) requires several steps. Often, the research problem and the sample go hand-in-hand. For some research projects, there may be several possible samples. The first question to ask yourself is: *Who can best answer the research questions posed in this study?* In the tradition of mixed methods research, more than one sample may be desirable. A common design is to administer a mail-out questionnaire to a large sample and to invite a smaller number of respondents to participate in telephone or face-to-face interviews. Conversely, interviews can be conducted first, followed by a larger-scale survey.

The sampling process begins by identifying the 'universe' of interest, for example, first-year university students, breast cancer survivors, or federal government employees. From this universe of participants, the sample is narrowed down by focusing on criteria such as location (e.g., country, region, city), demographic characteristics (e.g., age, gender, ethnicity/race of participants), and any other relevant criteria.

At this point, the sample is 'ideal'. The next step is to determine whether it is possible to study the desired sample. Ethical, political, financial, or sheer logistical considerations will affect the feasibility of constructing a sampling frame. Also, the availability of accurate lists containing names and contact information must be determined.

It is advisable to address the facets identified in this chapter and to read Chapter 6 before refining the sample any further. Many decisions made in subsequent facets of the research design will affect the final sample selection.

Completing behavioural ethics application(s) and anticipating political considerations

If you are a student attending a post-secondary institution and are conducting research on human 'subjects' – that is, your study participants – you will be required to gain approval for your research from your institution's behavioural research ethics board. Also, if you are conducting research at schools, hospitals, and other formal institutions, additional approvals may be required.

TEXT BOX 2.4

Ethics Alert!

Inform yourself early in the design of the study which ethics approvals you must obtain.

In addition, academic and professional bodies and associations (e.g., medical associations of a given country) are governed by specific codes of ethics that specify professional conduct including research. Behavioural ethics boards are interested in ensuring the following: respect for human dignity, free and informed consent, privacy and confidentiality, and minimal risk in relation to maximum benefit (Canadian Institutes of Health Research et al., 2010).

Some communities have developed their own culturally sensitive research protocols. For example, indigenous research protocols are based on the main principle that 'indigenous people should control their own knowledge; that they do their own research; and that if others choose to enter into any collaborative relationship with indigenous peoples the research should empower and benefit indigenous communities, not just researchers, their educational institutions, or society' (Battiste, 2007: 122). Sometimes traditional Western perspectives of what constitutes a research act are not in harmony with perspectives from other traditions. It is important to identify sources of disharmony in advance.

Research is an inherently political activity. Every aspect of a survey research project – including the nature of the question, gaining access to the research participants, securing funding, choosing the type of survey method, through to sharing the results of the research – may have a political dimension. Some topics may be simply taboo to research within certain environments. In addition, conflicts of interest may exacerbate political issues and must be identified *a priori*. Politics and ethics go hand-in-hand. Oftentimes, adhering to ethics guidelines raises political issues which will then require resolution.

In the initial formulation stages of a survey research project, it is important to (1) determine from whom ethics approval must be sought, (2) complete online ethics tutorials available from various research ethics bodies, (3) familiarize yourself with your institution's and, if appropriate, your discipline's and/or professional organization's codes of ethics, (4) learn how to locate application forms, and (5) determine how long the approval process takes. The design and execution of a survey research project should be guided by the principles of ethical and professional good practice. The topic of ethics is addressed throughout the chapters of this book.

Specifying the type(s) of survey instrument(s) to be employed

A wide variety of survey instruments are available to the survey researcher, including pen-and-paper questionnaires, telephone interviews, face-to-face interviews (either in person or via webcam), and internet surveys. The choice of instrument(s) depends on numerous considerations. At this point in the decision-making process, the following questions must be answered: *Who is the sample? How many people will be included in the study? Do they have access to a telephone or the internet? Are they inclined to respond to an internet survey? What is the nature of the questions to be answered? Are the questions closed-ended or is the purpose of the survey to also seek more in-depth information through open-ended questions? What is the desired length of the survey? How important is the presence of an interviewer who can clarify questions or probe for more detailed information? What is the budget and timeline for the project? Are there sufficient funds, for e.g., printing and mailing questionnaires, travel, and multiple follow-ups?*

It may be desirable to employ more than one type of data collection technique. As Fine and Weis (1996: 267) point out, 'methods are not passive strategies. They differently produce, reveal, and enable the display of different kinds of identities'. Often, survey research textbooks frame different types of responses to a particular mode of collection as problematic and suggest that remedial actions are required to ensure consistency (Dillman, 2000; Dillman et al., 1996; Payne, 1951). Although it is important to acknowledge that different modes may result in different responses, such differences can be considered a strength in that triangulation built into data collection will help to uncover how responses converge, are inconsistent, and/or are contradictory. In other words, a much more complex portrait of the lives lived by respondents can be painted by incorporating two or more methods of data collection into the design.

Determining what skills you will need

New survey researchers often neglect to consider in advance the skills they will need to complete their research projects. Survey research is both an art and a science and requires the researcher to possess a broad range of jack- or jill-of-all trades-like skills. This facet is devoted to identifying the analytical skills that you will require for a survey research project.

Most survey research projects require the manipulation of numbers and hence the employment of statistical software programs. Increasingly, survey researchers manipulate text gathered in open-ended questions on pen-and-paper or online surveys or through interviews conducted face-to-face, over the telephone, or via webcam. Survey researchers need to possess foundational skills in both quantitative and qualitative research. These skills can be obtained through course work at the senior undergraduate or graduate level at universities, or through courses offered through extension classes at university or non-university institutions. In addition, many software development companies offer free trial software, downloadable from their websites, and related tutorials. More extensive training can be undertaken from these companies or from national statistics organizations (e.g., Statistics Canada, Office for National Statistics).

Data analysis schools are offered at many universities, for example, the Essex Summer School in Social Science Data Analysis (UK); methods@manchester: research methods in the social sciences, Manchester University (UK); several programs at the Institute for Social Research at the University of Michigan (USA); the German Academic Exchange Service (DAAD); and summer schools sponsored by the European Science Foundation. Software companies such as SPSS, SAS, STATA, ATLAS.ti, and MAXQDA have online tutorials and offer workshops at various locations around the world. Also, the Khan Academy (http://www.khanacademy.org/) is a great site for the self-directed learner.

The cost of the various software packages should be built into the project's budget. A less expensive alternative is to use the free student or trial versions. However, these versions have reduced capacity, time restrictions (e.g., 30 days), or both, and may not be suitable for a large or longer-term project. Often, post-secondary institutions have site licences for popular analytical software.

In addition, for survey research projects with an interview component, it is imperative that all interviewers involved in data collection possess the necessary skills to conduct interviews. Interviewing is both an art and a science, and good training will include concrete techniques such as asking probing questions and interpersonal skills such as empathy. See Chapter 8 for an extended discussion on interviewing skills.

Designing the survey instrument(s)

Once all of the facets above have been considered, it is time to begin constructing the survey instrument(s). In fact, this process will have already begun in the process of reviewing the literature and examining instruments used in other studies. Some items from other survey instruments may be useful in their original form, or they can be modified to suit your study. Although most survey instruments are not copyrighted and other researchers are encouraged to use them, when feasible, it is a courtesy to contact the researcher of the original study and explain how you will be using her/his instrument or individual items. Such contact may lead to a further exchange of ideas or strategies. Also, incorporating existing survey items into your questionnaire allows for direct comparison with previous research. Some well-known survey items are copyrighted, and cannot be used without the permission of the author or/and a related fee. The Senate House Library, University of London (http://www.ull.ac.uk/subjects/psychology/psycscales.shtml) maintains a list of popular scales.

Several decisions regarding the way the questions are organized and sequenced, the choice of wording, the extent to which open-ended questions are included, and the overall length of the survey will depend on the intended recipient. If the sample is comprised of young children, these considerations, along with language and tone, will differ from that of a survey with adults as the sample. In addition, the survey design, including font size, graphics, and colour should be customized to be appealing to the intended audience.

Pre-contact information such as cover letters, consent forms, envelopes, and incentives will also need to be designed. These documents must conform to the requirements of the ethics bodies to which they must be submitted before the study can begin. Chapters 5 and 8 provide detailed accounts of survey design.

Specifying the sample and its size

Details of the sample must now be finalized. Will the sampling strategy be probabilistic, non-probabilistic, or both? Final determination of the sample size is made by considering issues of availability, accuracy, time, and costs. Compromises among what constitutes the ideal sample, what sample can realistically be constructed, and what is affordable in term of financial and temporal resources, are inevitable.

Devising a 'doable' schedule and budget

The creation of a research schedule and budget is an essential part of the survey design process. Survey research can be conducted with minimal costs, as in the case of some online surveys, or can be very expensive, for example mail surveys and related printing and postage costs or surveys where multiple interviewers are employed. When creating a budget, every expense should be documented, including the cost of analytical software and related training.

Equally careful attention should be paid to creating a schedule or timeline. In doing so, it is critical to be well versed in the ebb and flow of your sample's daily lives. That is, during certain periods, it is impossible or highly undesirable to try to administer a survey. For example, school boards may have moratoria on conducting research for several weeks at the beginning or end of each school term. Even if such moratoria do not exist, it would be unwise to try to administer a survey or conduct interviews during periods of intense activity or absences due to holidays or other events.

The research schedule should map out the entire range of survey research activity, beginning with initial formulation of the research question, through to completion of the final report, thesis, or dissertation. Although it should be highly structured, the schedule must also be flexible to allow for contingencies along the way (e.g., delays in getting ethics approval, a mail strike).

The creation of a budget and research schedule may provoke you to revisit and rethink the earlier facets in this chapter. See Chapter 8 for a more detailed discussion of budgets, schedules, and time management.

Piloting the instruments and training assistants

Throughout the survey development process, individual items and eventually the entire instrument will need to be piloted or pre-tested. The purpose of piloting is manifold: to ensure that the level of language used in the questions is appropriate and understandable to the audience; to assess whether the questions are understood as intended; to test different versions of a question; and to determine whether the order of questions is logical and skip instructions are correct (e.g., when respondents are instructed to go to a question other than the one that follows). In the case of surveys that are read, it is important to check whether the font size and type are easily readable by those who represent the target audience, and that the layout is appealing and engaging.

Questions and instruments can be piloted with experts on the topic of the survey and with focus groups. Pilot testing at this level will help to ensure that the content of the survey is accurate and that important topics and items have been included. Ultimately, the questions and questionnaire should always be piloted with those who share the same characteristics of the intended survey respondents. Piloting should be carried out well in advance to allow for revision and re-piloting.

In addition, at this point a coding scheme for data entry should be prepared. Defining the variables by giving them names and labels and specifying the value labels (e.g., 0 for a 'no' answer and 1 for a 'yes') will allow for the detection of problems with data analysis before the survey is administered. In the case of open-ended questions or interviews, at least some codes and themes can be generated *a priori*. Chapter 9 provides a detailed account of how to 'test-drive' your survey instrument(s) before they are administered.

If assistants are employed to conduct interviews, they must be trained carefully to ensure that they have strong communication skills, that they pose the questions as intended, that they keep accurate records of non-contact or refusal to participate, and they keep notes about any issues or problems that arise during the data collection phase. Also, it is important that interviewers understand the extent to which they should interact with respondents while conducting an interview.

Administering the survey

Finally, it is time to administer the survey! How this facet is enacted depends on the nature of the survey, details of which are specified in Chapter 8. It is important to have a detailed plan and ensure that it is followed. For example, in the case of mail-out surveys, the timing of subsequent follow-ups is crucial. Any mid-course changes to the sampling or survey administration procedure must be considered carefully, as a careless change could invalidate the integrity of the study. At all times, the confidentiality of the sample must be maintained and ethics requirements upheld. Record-keeping throughout the data collection process is essential to determine response and non-response rates, and unreachable respondents. In Chapter 8 the topic of survey administration is expanded.

Anticipating data coding and clean-up

Although the topic of data analysis is beyond the scope of this book, anticipating data coding and clean-up is part of the survey design process. Earlier, I suggested that a coding scheme should be prepared during the piloting facet. In addition, a plan for cleaning-up the data should be anticipated. That is, often data are entered incorrectly and the survey researcher must ensure that such errors are corrected. Software, such as Microsoft Access, can be used to eliminate many errors.

Also, it is necessary to specify a plan for analysing open-ended questions or interview data. It may be desirable to develop coding schemes in advance, as informed by the theoretical framework of the study. Or text may be coded inductively. Again, you must assess what skills you need to carry out the analyses. More details of this facet are presented in Chapter 9.

Preparing for analysis

When all of the data have been collected, it is time to prepare the final report, thesis, or dissertation. It is important to build adequate time for manuscript completion into your schedule, as this task usually takes much longer than anticipated. Again, you need to determine whether you possess the skills needed to complete the report, and if not, how to go about acquiring these skills. Also, the analytical methods that are appropriate for the data at hand should be reassessed. Finally, you should remind yourself of the audience, any related guidelines or requirements. In the case of a thesis or dissertation, it is important to check the requirements of the institution. Preparing for analysis is addressed in more detail in Chapter 9.

Summary

In this chapter, the entire survey research design process has been mapped out. A chart specifying each facet of design was presented and the interrelatedness of the facets was highlighted. Careful attention to the design of each facet specified in this chapter will result in a strong survey research study.

Exercise

1 Replicate Figure 2.1 on a large sheet of paper. Brainstorm in as much detail as possible about each facet of the survey research design process. Make detailed notes for each facet. Throughout this brainstorming exercise, note any strengths, questions, concerns, contradictions, and/or ethical issues that arise.

Further reading

Battiste, M. (2007). Research ethics for protecting indigenous knowledge and heritage: Instutional and researcher responsibilities. In N. K. Denzin and M. D. Giardina (eds), *Ethical Futures in Qualitative Research. Decolonizing the Politics of Knowledge.* Walnut Creek, CA: Left Coast Press.

Fine, M., Weis, L., Weseen, S., and Wong, L. (2000). For whom? Qualitative research, representations, and social responsibilities. In N. K. Denzin and Y. S. Lincoln (eds), *Handbook of Qualitative Research* (2nd edition). Thousand Oaks, CA: Sage.

Mathison, S. (1988). Why triangulate? *Educational Researcher*, 17(2), 13–17.

THREE

Conceptualizing your survey research study

Regardless of the format(s) employed, all survey research projects begin by stating the purpose of the study, specifying research questions, and developing survey items to be administered during the data collection phase. It is critical to conceptualize, from the outset, the logic of an entire survey research project, as outlined in Chapter 2. In this chapter I focus on the formulation of concepts, conceptual models, and related analytical models in relation to the research questions. The roles of exogenous and endogenous variables, latent constructs and indicator variables, dependent and independent variables, and variables as mediators and moderators in survey research are explained. This rather detailed discussion of concepts and various ways of thinking about variables is intended to prompt you to anticipate carefully how you will analyse your data. Without carefully considering the concepts, constructs, and indicators that emerge from your research interests and questions, you may neglect to include one or more key indicator variables. As a result, you will be unable to formulate or analyse key constructs that are critical to your research.

Formulating research problems

One central task in the survey research endeavour is to concretize abstract and directly unmeasurable concepts such as 'love' or 'happiness' into measurable indicators in the form of survey items. The ultimate goal is to generate a data set – in the form of numbers, words, or both – from these measurable indicators in order to answer your research questions. The formulation of concepts and research questions is an iterative task. Initial questions will suggest certain concepts. As you become better informed about the nature of concepts and their related measures, you will be able to sharpen your research questions and their related concepts.

The process of conceptualizing the study goes hand-in-hand with the other facets of the study, such as specifying the sample, itemizing the budget, and determining time restraints. In Chapter 2, I identified 'using triangulation to determine what is already known' as one of the facets of survey research design. The conceptualization process begins by engaging with multiple sources – theory, methods, data collection strategies, analytical techniques – to help identify and clarify the key concepts in your research project. A good place to start is by reading the existing literature. Once you have identified an initial topic or research question, a triangulation strategy can be employed to engage with the literature. Throughout this process, you will read for different reasons. These reasons include learning about different theoretical perspectives, sharpening your conceptual definitions, defining variables to be included on your survey instrument, looking for examples of exemplary studies, and learning from less than stellar work to improve your research study. By reading widely within your given discipline and across disciplines, the literature can be scrutinized for evidence of *convergence, inconsistency*, and *contradiction* (Mathison, 1988; as described in Chapter 2) of conceptual perspectives and their related definitions and measures. Existing survey instruments can be examined to determine how certain concepts have been measured. Unclear or illogical conceptualization can be identified, along with gaps in the literature or recommendations for further research.

The assistance of a research librarian is invaluable at this point. S/he will help you clarify the key concepts and narrow your research to a manageable size, the 'just right' Goldilocks approach as suggested by Blaxter et al. (2010). Also, search engines such as Google Scholar and its email alert function will help you stay abreast of new research. Conversations with key informants will help you think about the key issues and topics for your research. Finally, conversations with individuals who are similar to your final survey project will help you refine and sharpen your study. After having completed an initial investigation, you will be ready to start identifying the concepts that you will include in your research.

What are concepts?

Concepts are mental images, labels, or symbols for ideas of central importance to your research. Denzin (1989) describes concepts as empirical *sensitizers*. Concepts are not real, but rather are socially constructed based on the researcher's life experiences, perspectives specific to a particular academic discipline, and engagement with the theoretical literature. An elegant definition of concept is provided by Bollen (1989: 180): 'A concept is an idea that unites phenomena (e.g., attitudes, behaviours, traits) under a single term … [A] concept … acts as a summarizing device to replace a list of specific traits that an individual may exhibit'.

Cartoon 3.1

A survey research project often begins with labels that loosely define concepts. Sometimes, relationships among concepts are also suggested. For instance, you may be interested in 'identities, ethnic origin, and success at university', 'healthy food choices and perceptions of self', or 'marriage patterns and financial well-being'. All of the labels will automatically trigger mental images but without clear definitions, and these images will vary across individuals. For example, the term 'marriage' is abstract in that for one person it may mean a religiously sanctioned union between a woman and a man, while for another person it may mean any long-term partnership in which the couple consider themselves to be in a married or marriage-like relationship. In other words, concepts are often vague, abstract, and complex. They must be concretized or *operationalized* in order to measure and analyse them and produce meaningful results from them.

Concretization or *operationalization* takes different forms, depending on whether you use closed-ended questions, open-ended questions, or both, with the purpose of either measuring variation or tapping more deeply into the meaning of a given concept. When the goal is to use close-ended items that can be converted into numerical values, it is the role of the survey researcher to convert these abstract images into measureable entities, most often called *variables*. This process is deductive in nature. That is, nominal and operational definitions and related hypotheses are provided for each variable, and specific measures are devised to measure them. When the goal is to use open-ended questions to further understand the meaning of a concept or its dimensions, developing precise survey items *a priori* is not necessary. Rather, *codes* in qualitative software packages are the equivalent of variables and serve a similar purpose. However, data, in the form of words, will be analysed inductively. That is, after the data collection process, the words and phrases themselves will then be converted inductively into some set of items by grouping them into themes. The various grouped responses can also be quantified by assigning numerical values to them, which can, in turn, be analysed in a similar manner to closed-ended survey items. Whether employing closed or open-ended questions to study phenomena, the goal is to examine the extent of variation in responses. In other words, we want to assess the degree to which individuals respond similarly or differently to a given question.

Through an investigation of the literature and by talking with librarians, informed colleagues, and conducting focus groups, the concepts will be sharpened, focused and delimited to the point that clear and unambiguous definitions can be provided. The following three steps can be followed to define concepts and to either create variables to measure them or to construct open-ended questions to probe more deeply into the variety of meanings that respondents attribute to some of the concepts.

Specifying a nominal definition for each concept

By conducting literature reviews and consulting formally and informally with colleagues and those who are similar to your intended respondents, eventually you will be able to provide a clear and precise definition for each concept in your survey research project. This nominal (also called theoretical or constitutional) definition will require you to make decisions regarding what theoretical perspectives to embrace. Decisions may be influenced by the ideological stance or disciplinary protocols of your research team or committee or yourself. Also, ethical considerations may influence the way a concept is defined. For example, in a study about pain, it may be ideal from a pure research sense for the researcher to inflict pain on research participants and then question them about the degree of sensation experienced. Ethically, this approach is most likely to be considered unacceptable. Instead, questions that ask respondents to reflect back on instances of pain are a more ethically acceptable approach.

In academic research, nominal definitions must be defensible as being sound from a theoretical perspective. Standard definitions, such as those used on the census of a given country, may be employed for some concepts such as 'occupation'. Other well-defined concepts such as 'locus of control' may also be employed, but due to copyright issues, you may be required to obtain permission to use these types of measurement scales. If your goal is to extend current theoretical understandings, then you will want to create new or expanded definitions for concepts. Competing or complementary definitions also serve to further extend our theoretical understandings. Definitions serve to clarify and focus each concept. By defining a concept you are better able to create indicators in order to measure it.

Specifying the dimensions of a concept

Because concepts in the social sciences are complex, they may be multi-dimensional. That is, they may include more than one type of central idea or image and hence need to labelled accordingly. For example, in my research on the educational destinations of young people, I began with Pierre Bourdieu's theory of reproduction and his two related concepts of social and cultural reproduction. This led to the development of two specific concepts: 'parents as sources of cultural capital' and 'parents as sources of social capital'. In their analysis of the concept of 'justice', Ruitenberg and Vokey (2010) identified four dimensions: justice as 'harmony', as 'equality', as 'equity', and as 'difference'. An empirical analysis of justice would require four different distinct sets of measures for each concept. The broader concept of 'justice' serves as an overarching dimension under which the four more specific constructs are subsumed. By specifying the four dimensions of justice, they each become uni-dimensional; that is, they each measure just one thing.

At this point, even when definitions are provided, concepts remain rather abstract. The next step is to specify specific measures of a concept.

Creating concrete measures of a concept

The nature of the question will determine the extent to which a specific measure of a concept is operationalized. When the goal is to generate numbers in order to analyse data quantitatively, it is necessary to develop closed-ended questions – that is, items that require 'yes/no' answers, or answers to scales such as 'strongly agree, agree, disagree, strongly disagree' (see Chapter 5 for a comprehensive discussion of questions and their related scales). When the goal is to probe for the meanings and understandings of respondents without supplying a fixed set of responses, only questions or statements used to elicit such responses need to be developed.

Measures of closed-ended survey items

In survey research, the definitions used to define a concept must be further concretized into specific measurable indicators. This is called providing *operational* – that is functionally usable – definitions of a concept. In the terminology of survey research, the *stem* (the part of the item that poses a question or statement) and a finite number of *response categories* must be developed. Several considerations are necessary when developing specific indicators. First, the measures must be as closely associated to concepts as possible. Often, it is useful to have multiple indicators of a concept in order to conduct more sophisticated and rich data analyses. Second, the type of scale employed must be suitable for a given measure.

Measures of open-ended survey items

Open-ended survey questions require only the stem part of the question or statement. Because respondents supply their own responses, fixed response categories are not required. However, the degree to which open-ended questions are developed will depend on the survey format employed. Self-administered surveys such as pen-and-paper questionnaires are limited to the extent to which they can include probing questions beyond the open-ended question. However, with interviewer-administered surveys, it is possible for the interviewer to formulate additional questions based on the interviewee's responses as the interview proceeds.

Survey research, like all research, is an iterative process. The research questions that you have identified before having gone through the exercise of specifying and defining concepts, followed by providing operational definitions for specific indicators, need to be revisited and revised.

Hypotheses

In the simplest sense, hypotheses are educated guesses. From the very initial stages of a study, informal hypotheses drive our decision-making. Is happiness the same as well-being? Are the two concepts related or do they suggest different phenomena? Will members of different cultural groups hold different views about what constitutes happiness, well-being, or both? Do men respond differently than women to questions about happiness and well-being? Although all these questions could be called research questions, in order to formulate them a series of educated guesses is required about what is and what is not worthwhile to pursue.

In some research circles, 'hypothesis' is a dirty word that implies strict testing of theory. Those conducting research that is deemed to be inductive, that is, starting from the concrete and leading to the abstract, prefer to assert that their approach is hypothesis-free. As we do not engage in value-free research, neither do we engage in hypothesis-free research. Without at least informal hypotheses,

Cartoon 3.2

we could never confirm what we suspected, nor could we be surprised about unexpected findings. Nor could we create stems to open-ended questions such as 'Describe, in your own words, what daily events, encounters, and activities contribute to your overall well-being'. This stem contains hypotheses about the sorts of phenomena that are associated with happiness, that there is something called 'overall well-being' and that respondents will vary more or less in their written responses to this statement.

In other circles, narrow, precisely-stated hypotheses are considered essential for specifying the nature, direction, and strength of relationships of constructs and variables in a study in order to conduct analyses, with the intention of 'rejecting' or 'failing to reject' the stated hypotheses. In the latter case, our theoretical understandings which informed the selection of concepts, and related constructs and indicator variables, will provide structured guidance to make educated guesses about the nature, direction, and strength of relationships.

The degree to which hypotheses are stated explicitly is often dictated by disciplinary and paradigmatic traditions. Regardless of the extent to which hypotheses are formally structured and articulated, it is a useful exercise for all researchers to consider in advance how concepts and related variables (in a quantitative sense) or codes (in a qualitative sense) are related or interrelated.

Constructs and indicators

Once the concepts for the study have been delineated, they need to be operationalized further into measureable items. In the next section, through the use of an example from Andres (2009), I describe the various types of variables.

How scientists propose

Cartoon 3.3

Latent variables or constructs

Latent constructs or variables emerge from the concept formulation exercise. By refining and focusing concepts, latent constructs are more concrete in that they have the potential to be measured. However, they remain abstract in that they cannot be measured directly and remain unobserved or unmeasured (Bollen, 1989: 11). However, the specification of latent constructs signals the shift from a theoretical or conceptual model to an analytical model. The convention for depicting a latent construct is by a circle. All of the variables in the circles in Figure 3.1 are latent constructs in that they cannot be measured directly.

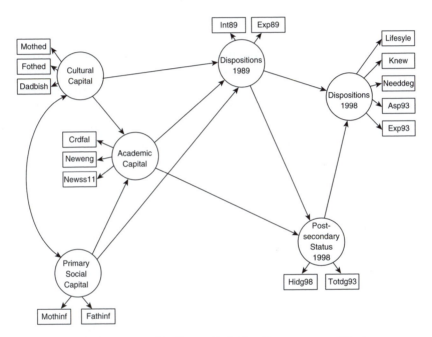

Figure 3.1 Model of Latent and Indicator Variables, Exogenous and Endogenous Variables, and Independent and Dependent Variables

Andres, L. (2009). The cumulative impact of capital and identity construction across time: A fifteen year perspective of Canadian young women and men. In K. Robson and C. Sanders (eds), *Quantifying theory: Bourdieu.* Berlin: Springer. Reproduced with the kind permission of Springer. All rights reserved.

Indicator variables

Indicator variables, also called manifest variables, are concrete measures used to collect information through survey research. In other words, indicator variables can be observed in that they are measurable through items on a questionnaire or in a survey interview. Definitions associated with the latent constructs will shape the development of indicator variables. Indicator variables are specified in path models as rectangles, as in Figure 3.1. The arrows linking them with a latent variable indicate that they 'load' onto the construct and hence serve as one or more measures of a latent variable.

Exogenous and endogenous variables

An *exogenous* variable is outside the model in the sense that no attempt is made to explain its variability within the analysis. For example, the latent variables 'cultural capital' and 'primary social capital' in Figure 3.1 are exogenous. Other exogenous variables may also appear in such models, but they will either be free-standing or, at most, correlated with other exogenous variables. *Endogenous* variables are 'inside' the model and the goal of analysis is to explain their variability by their relations with other exogenous and endogenous variables contained in the model. All of the other constructs and their related measures in Figure 3.1 are endogenous variables. Exogenous and endogenous variables are used in causal or structural equation modelling. These terms are also useful in conceptualizing survey research that will be analysed using other types of analysis.

Dependent and independent variables

The goal in most empirical research is to explain the variability or spread of values on the key variables of interest. The *dependent* variable is an outcome or response variable. The ultimate dependent latent variable in Figure 3.1 is 'dispositions 1998'. That is, the goal is to explain variability of the *dependent* variable. The spread of values is caused, predicted or influenced by other variables, called *independent* variables. The latent variables 'academic capital', 'dispositions 1989', and 'post-secondary status 1998' are both dependent and independent in the model in Figure 3.1.

Variables as mediators

A mediating variable is one that comes between – or mediates – an independent variable and a dependent variable. It is also called an intervening variable. While it may be hypothesized that independent variable A will have a direct effect or influence on variable C, there may also be a direct relationship between variable A and variable B, and between variable B and variable C. Through the causal path $A \rightarrow B \rightarrow C$, the relationship between variable A and C is indirect. Through

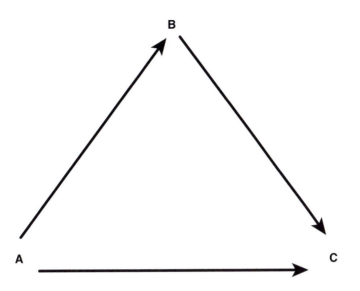

Figure 3.2 Mediator Variable Model

the causal path $A \rightarrow C$, the relationship is direct. Using the terms 'independent' and 'dependent' introduced above, in the $A \rightarrow C$ relationship, A is the independent variable and C is the dependent variable. In the $A \rightarrow B \rightarrow C$ causal path, A remains independent in relation to B and C; B is independent of C, and C is dependent on B. However, B is dependent on A. Hence, B is both independent and dependent in this small model.

Models can include more than one mediating variable. Mediating variables can take the form of indicators in the case of simple path modelling, or of latent constructs in the more sophisticated structural equation modelling. The latent variables 'academic capital', 'dispositions 1989', and 'post-secondary status 1998' are mediating variables in Figure 3.1. Mediating variables add complexity to theoretical and analytical models, and hence enhance the explanatory power of our research.

Variables as moderators

Moderator variables do not cause, lead to, or influence direct effects or indirect effects. For example, being female does not cause more happiness or result in better reading scores. Rather, variables such as sex, geographic region, or age group – variables Q, R, and S in Figure 3.3 – can be subdivided into different levels and the relationship between an independent variable A and dependent variable B may differ based on the level of such moderator variables.

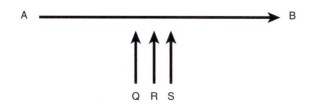

Figure 3.3 Moderator Variable Model

Moderator variables are often demographic or contextual in nature (e.g., sex, geographic region, age). Using these examples, it can be hypothesized that the relationship between an independent and dependent variable may be moderated by levels of, for example, sex (e.g., female and male), geographic region (e.g., metropolitan, urban/rural, remote), or age group (e.g., the 19–25 age category versus the 26–34 age category). Moderating variables are not depicted in path models such as Figure 3.3. Rather, data are analysed by the levels of a moderating variable of interest.

A moderator variable is sometimes used to demonstrate an interaction effect in that the relationship between *A* and *B* in Figure 3.3 may vary across the levels of one or more of the moderator variables *Q, R, S*. However, using techniques such as structural equation modelling, analyses can be conducted by initially constraining the analysis to one group and then unconstraining the model by one or more moderators to determine whether significant differences exist.

Theoretical and analytical models can contain both mediator and moderator variables. Some types of variables, such as sex or geographic region, are always moderators. However, other variables can be mediators in some analyses and moderators in other analyses. A variable cannot, however, be a mediator and moderator in the same analysis. Also, mediation and moderation can be combined to create *mediated moderation* and *moderated mediation* models. See Edwards (2007) for an extended discussion of these combinations, as well as Baron and Kenny (1986) and Holmbeck (1997) for a more extended discussion of mediators and moderators.

Types of relationships

Survey research is versatile in that it produces data that can be analysed in a myriad of ways. Often, relationships between or among variables are considered to be statistical in nature. These analyses include frequencies, crosstabulation, analysis of variance, factor analysis, correlation, regression analysis, correspondence analysis, hierarchical linear modelling, and causal or structural equation modelling. However, data produced from open-ended questions which lend themselves, at least initially, to qualitative analyses will also be analysed to assess differences between groups and associations among codes. The qualitative software program ATLAS.ti has a 'network view' feature that allows for the examination of many different types of association such as the relationship between C1 (code 1) and C2 (code 2). The relationships can be specified as follows: 'associated with', 'a part of', 'a cause of', 'contradicts', 'is a', and/or 'is a property of' (Muhr and Friese, 2004).

Precisely because of the versatility of data generated from survey research, it is beyond the scope of this text to provide an in-depth discussion of analytical techniques. I strongly advise you as a student of survey research to seek out training in both quantitative and qualitative analytical methods in order to learn the range of analytical tools you will need to tackle the analyses most suitable to your data. The many books by Norušis (e.g., 2012) provide a readable and thorough introduction to statistics. For a concise summary of multivariate statistics and the types of questions they seek to answer, see Schutz (1983); and for an extended but accessible discussion of multivariate analyses, see Tabachnick and Fidell (2006). For a discussion of relationships unique to qualitative analysis, see Marshall and Rossman (2006), Merriam et al. (2001), and the ATLAS.ti manual (Muhr and Friese, 2004). Mixed methods texts, such as those by Bergman (2008a), Cresswell et al. (2008), and Tashakkori and Teddlie (2008), provide extensive discussions on combining quantitative and qualitative perspectives in research projects.

Summary

This chapter commenced with a description of the conceptualization process. After having reviewed the literature, consulted with experts on your topic, held focus-group discussions, and discussed the study with individuals who are similar to the intended sample, concepts and related constructs will begin to emerge. Descriptions of nominal definitions and related dimensions of concepts were highlighted. Also, hypotheses and the various types of variables were described.

Exercises

1 Refine your research problem by conducting a literature review, talking with experts, holding focus-group sessions, and talking with individuals who are similar to your intended sample(s).

2 Define the relevant concepts and their related dimensions for your study.

3 Provide nominal definitions for each of the constructs.

4 Specify all the variables for your study. Identify each variable as latent, indicator, independent, dependent, exogenous, and/or endogenous.

5 Specify the research hypotheses by specifying the nature, direction, and strength of the relationships among your variables.

6 Attempt to design a model for your study. Provide both a schematic model and a written description. Specify the dependent variable(s), key independent variables, and all mediating and moderating variables contained in your model.

Further reading

Baron, R. M., and Kenny, D. A. (1986) The moderator-mediator variable distinction in social psychological research: Conceptual, strategic, and statistical considerations. *Journal of Personality and Social Psychology*, 51(6), 1173–1182.
Bollen, K. A. (1989) *Structural Equations with Latent Variables*. New York: Wiley.
Pedhazur, E. J. (1982) *Multiple Regression in Behavioral Research. Explanation and Prediction*. New York: Holt, Rinehart, and Winston.

FOUR
Survey formats

'Survey research' is an umbrella term under which a variety of different formats for gathering information reside. You have surely completed numerous pen-and-paper questionnaires and have participated in the occasional telephone interview. You have probably completed an online survey. Although each format has its own distinct features, advantages, and disadvantages, there are several commonalities among them. Each format is designed to solicit responses from individuals by asking questions or asking for responses to statements. The success of any format in terms of response rate depends on the salience of the topic, the sampling strategy employed, the wording and sequence of questions, the timing of administration, the ease of participation for the respondent, and the degree to which the respondent trusts that the data will be reported anonymously. However, each of these dimensions can be enhanced further by choosing the most suitable format and by combining formats in order to elicit the richest set of responses possible.

Mixed mode versus mixed methods designs

When considering which survey format(s) to employ, it is important to distinguish between two different perspectives, and perhaps two competing goals. The first perspective is that of *mixed modes* (Dillman, 2000). In a mixed mode approach, more than one survey format or mode is utilized with the goal of enhancing response rates. Each survey format has advantages and disadvantages, and potential respondents may vary in their preference of one format over the other. However, several studies have revealed that the nature and quality of responses may vary according to the survey format employed. As a result, data collected in one format may contradict or be incompatible with data collected in another format (de Leeuw, 1992; Dillman, 2000). For survey researchers who strive for consistency and who aim to avoid 'the unsettling problem that people's answers to any particular question vary depending on the survey mode' (Dillman, 2000: 6), measures must be undertaken to minimize the effect of the format on the responses. Dillman proposes a *unimode construction*. That is, when two or more formats are employed with the purpose of enhancing response rates and reducing non-consistent responses, the questions should be designed to provide the same mental stimulus, regardless of format. Attention to the consistency of response options, sequencing of questions, and instructions for completion will serve to reduce differences among different survey formats. For a more detailed discussion of unimode survey construction and related examples, see Dillman (2000) and de Leeuw and Hox (2008).

For researchers advocating a *mixed methods* approach to research, the goal is to embrace rather than stifle potentially contradictory findings collected by more than one method. Simply defined as taking 'the best of qualitative and quantitative methods and combin[ing] them' (Bergman, 2008c), mixed methods research strives to transcend the barriers erected by the tenets of the qualitative and quantitative research camps. The goal is to be purposefully 'unsettling' by designing studies that employ at least one quantitative and one qualitative method and related data analyses appropriate to the purpose and context of the study. True mixed methods research goes beyond having two or more methods that simply co-reside in a research project. Analyses from mixed methods designs endeavour to integrate the findings from the methods employed; hence, the resulting research findings should be greater than the sum of their quantitative and qualitative parts (Bryman, 2008; Tashakkori and Teddlie, 2008). Creative qualitative/quantitative configurations such as *triangulation, concurrent embedded, explanatory, exploratory*, and *sequential embedded* designs allow for the simultaneous merging of data or the use of one or more sources of data to extend the findings of research gathered by another method (Cresswell et al., 2008). Because data existing naturally under the rubric of survey research can be collected either quantitatively, qualitatively, or both, and hence can be analysed both qualitatively and quantitatively, mixed methods designs can be created easily by combining two or more modes. Moreover, data collected qualitatively can be quantified and data collected with the goal of conducting mainly quantitative analyses can include open-ended questions that can be analysed both qualitatively, quantitatively, or both (see Chapter 9). Conversely, one or more survey research formats can be incorporated into, for example, ethnographic or experimental research designs with the goals of strengthening the explanatory power of the findings.

Both unimode constructions and mixed methods designs should be kept in mind when considering what format(s) to employ in your survey project. Also, both perspectives could be adopted in a single project. For example, response rates to a mail survey could be enhanced by telephone follow-ups constructed in a unimode fashion which are designed to elicit, as far as possible, the same responses as the mail survey. Then, in the spirit of mixed methods research, face-to-face interviews could be conducted to complement, complete, further develop, expand, corroborate/confirm, compensate for, and/or diversify the findings of the first phase of the study (Tashakkori and Teddlie, 2008).

All survey research is subsumed under two formats: self-administered surveys and interviewer-administered surveys. Each of these formats has advantages and disadvantages.

Self-administered surveys

A self-administered survey format requires that the individual complete the survey unaided by an interviewer. Respondents are required to read, either on paper or on a computer, a set of items to which they are invited to respond; hence, they are presented with a 'visual channel of communication' (Weisberg, 2005: 32).

Self-administered surveys have several advantages. In most instances, respondents are able to complete the survey at their own leisure. As a result, responses may be more thoughtful and reflective. Sometimes, in order to respond to certain questions the respondent must consult records (e.g., university transcripts, sources of investment income). The ability to do so in a self-administered format will lead to greater accuracy, and hence better quality of information reported. Visual aids, such as charts, can be included in self-administered surveys. Because the respondent is not confronted with having to disclose information to an interviewer, a self-administered survey mode is more conducive to studies on sensitive topics. Surveys that are read can employ longer lists of similar questions and can be constructed with more and/or more complex response categories.

There are a few disadvantages associated with self-administered surveys. The respondent must be able to read the survey, follow the instructions, and respond as accurately as possible. Adaptation of survey instruments for certain groups (e.g., children, non-native language speakers, those with low literacy skills) may be possible. Otherwise, another format will be more appropriate. Because an interviewer is not involved in the data collection process, all components of the survey instrument must be clear, straightforward, and unambiguous. In addition, in a self-administered format, there is no guarantee that the survey instrument has been completed by the intended respondent.

There is some evidence that respondents to self-administered surveys are less likely to provide detailed answers to open-ended questions (Czaja and Blair, 2005: 39), leading to the conclusion that 'open answers often do not produce useful data' (Fowler, 2009: 72). However, others provide contradictory findings.

For example, de Leeuw (1992) conducted an analysis of differences in responses to open-ended questions by mode (mail, face-to-face and telephone) and reported that differences were small and varied by type and position of the question. In my own experience, individuals do provide detailed responses to open-ended questions. For example, in the 22-year follow-up to my longitudinal study of the 1988 high school graduates, 90% of the 573 respondents to the self-administered mail-out survey provided written responses to the open-ended question asking them to explain their answers to a set of Likert-type questions on the extent to which the 2008 financial crisis had affected them. In total, 44 pages of open-ended data were produced from this question (Andres, 2010). The extent to which respondents provide responses to open-ended questions depends on the relevance of the topic.

Group administered surveys

When surveys are administered in a group format, the sample is almost always some type of intact convenience sample. For example, individuals in a classroom setting or participants partaking in a bus tour are intact 'convenient' groups to which surveys can be administered *en masse*. Minimal costs, the ability to identify samples in advance, ease of administration, and the speed at which the surveys can be administered are the advantages of this format. Also, non-responses are usually reduced to those who are absent at the time of administration.

Although this format is primarily self-administered via pen and paper, the surveyor must at least deliver and collect the surveys and provide a minimum amount of explanation regarding their completion. Often, the surveyor invigilates the completion of the survey. It is possible that the surveyor, through the instructions or information about the purpose of the survey, could influence how the surveys are completed. The group setting, too, may create an atmosphere that affects how respondents give their answers.

Because of these potential disadvantages, the surveyor administering a group survey must pay attention to the instructions provided to the group, how questions by respondents will be answered, and whether and how those who are absent will be followed up. To ensure that surveys are completed fully and thoughtfully, sufficient time must be provided for their completion.

Mail surveys

Mail surveys are pen-and-paper surveys that are delivered to respondents by post or by courier. The respondent is instructed to return the surveys using the prepaid addressed envelope that should be provided. A mail survey has a certain charm in that it is a tangible entity. The accompanying cover letter can be personalized by addressing the intended respondent by name and can be signed personally by the surveyor. Cover letters can add an air of legitimacy and authority if they are produced on official stationary and are signed or co-signed by a person of authority. Mail questionnaires can be made attractive through interesting graphics, colour schemes, illustrations, and choice of font. Font sizes and style can be adjusted to suit the audience. Also, incentives of various forms (e.g., fridge magnets, sticky notes, pens, USB sticks) can be included in the survey package, along with research reports, newsletters, or other information of interest to the respondents.

All the advantages of self-administered surveys are present in mail surveys. In addition, for the most part, mail surveys are not constrained by geographical boundaries; however, mail services to and from some countries may be problematic. Depending on the intended audience, it is possible for mail surveys to be longer and more complex than is advisable with other formats.

In addition to the general disadvantages of self-administered surveys, mail surveys are rather expensive. Costs include the printing of questionnaires, mail envelopes, return envelopes, and reminder postcards; the price of postage; the cost of incentives and other enclosures; preparation of the mail-out packages; follow-up of undeliverables and non-respondents; and entry of data. Mail surveys require a sampling frame for which up-to-date mailing lists are available, as inaccurate mailing lists will drive up the costs of survey administration.

Because the administration of mail surveys requires administration and follow-up through the mail, when compared with other methods, the overall time to conduct such studies may be eight weeks or longer. After the initial mail-out, non-respondents are sent reminder postcards. For undeliverable surveys, additional attempts to track down current mailing addresses may be attempted. After another waiting time period, a second survey package will be sent out, perhaps followed up with another reminder card or telephone call.

Because the survey is self-administered and because individuals complete the surveys at their leisure, low response rates may result. A salient research topic, a compelling cover letter and detailed related completion instructions, a well-crafted survey instrument, appropriate incentives and enclosures, and diligent follow-ups will increase the response rates.

Diaries

Diaries are a form of mail survey where respondents are asked to record, in considerable detail and usually over a period of time (e.g., a week or a month), certain behaviours. Examples of recordable behaviours are television viewing patterns, exercising and eating behaviours.

In addition, by employing panel designs – that is, designs following the same people over time – and a survey structure designed specifically to record autobiographical memory, calendars and time diaries can be used to document the life courses of individuals. That is, information about educational and occupational attainment, marriage and family formation, and well-being and happiness can be captured over time through the use of diaries. Calendars are used to record the timing and duration of events, 'states, conditions, and/or activities' (Belli et al., 2009: 5) in the distant past, that is, months or years ago, and time diaries are employed to collect these types of information about the immediate past – the last day or week (Belli et al., 2009).

Online surveys

The use of online surveys has increased dramatically over the past several years. However, there are several drawbacks to online surveys, the most important being that of coverage issues (see Chapter 7 for coverage errors). Although more and more individuals have access to computers and the internet, coverage and usage are not as predictable as opening one's mail or answering the telephone. Some individuals are connected constantly to the internet, while others may have access only at their work places. Others may check their email only sporadically. Internet use is correlated with age, educational status, income levels, and race/ethnicity, so online surveys are not likely to be appropriate when the frame population is comprised of, for example, senior citizens. Those living in geographically remote areas may have limited or no internet service. Also, although in theory the world of internet users is unlimited geographically, individuals in some countries or specific regions within countries may be difficult or impossible to reach through the internet. As the number of smart phone users and smart phone survey formats increases worldwide, so will the possibilities of reaching a wider audience over the internet.

Because email addresses are required of the frame population, online surveys work best when non-sampling coverage error is known to be minimal. Individuals within intact organizations such as municipal offices, student bodies, and employees in large companies where internet use is part of everyday working life are good candidates for online surveys.

Once it is deemed appropriate to use an online survey, there are many advantages beyond those of self-administered surveys described earlier in this chapter. Online surveys are inexpensive to administer and, because they do not require the use of paper, they are environmentally sound. It is possible to collect data very quickly. Follow-up of non-respondents can be done easily over email.

There are two types of online surveys: email surveys and web surveys. Each is described below.

Email Surveys

An email survey is the more primitive and basic form of online survey. Survey instruments are either embedded in the body of an email message or created in a word-processing program and attached to an email message. Respondents are sent email messages describing the purpose of the survey and other related details – the email equivalent of a cover letter – followed by directions for completing and returning the survey.

There are several advantages to email surveys. They can be administered quickly and easily and, depending on the characteristics of the intended respondents, may be completed and returned quickly. Email surveys are the least expensive of all surveys as there are no printing, mailing, or interviewer-related costs. Survey administration software and web hosting are not required.

However, there are several disadvantages. Surveys embedded in emails must be kept simple. Formatting is often difficult for surveys within an email message as different email programs will align text and response categories in unintended ways. The sequencing of skip questions cannot be programmed to occur automatically. Also, the resulting data must be entered manually.

Coverage errors may remain a problem in that many email programs have filters to flag unsolicited messages as junk mail. Some filters will not accept bulk mail emails. Recipients may simply delete the message as email surveys are becoming overused. Surveys returned via the emails of the respondents are not anonymous; hence, email surveys may not be the best format for collecting sensitive data. Response rates are reported to be lower than for web surveys (Sue and Ritter, 2007: 8)

Web surveys

Individuals are usually invited to participate in a web survey initially through email contact. A 'cover letter' sent by email will describe the study and provide a web link to the web survey. In order to ensure that surveys are completed only once by each respondent, a PIN number and password are provided. Potential respondents can gain access to the web survey at their leisure and complete it in one or more sessions.

Web surveys have all the advantages of self-administered surveys and email surveys. In addition, there are several added bonuses. Web surveys can be technologically sophisticated in that audio streaming, video streaming, or both can be embedded within the instrument. The sequencing of questions can be programmed to provide a seamless series of questions. For example, if the first question of the survey is 'Over the past five years, have you attended a post-secondary institution?', for those who answer 'yes' the correct sequence of questions will appear and those who answered 'no' will be directed automatically to the appropriate section of the survey. Data collection can be conducted automatically, which eliminates both the cost of data entry and any human errors.

There is an abundance of commercial web hosting services and increasingly they are becoming more user-friendly. Survey researchers with a minimum of technical expertise can design and administer their own surveys. Conversely, more extensive technical assistance can be purchased from commercial web hosting services for a fee. Sue and Ritter (2007) provide an extensive set of criteria to consider when choosing a web hosting service. In addition, they provide an exhaustive list of web hosting services, which, unfortunately, is limited to those available in the USA.

The disadvantages of web surveys beyond those of self-administered and email surveys are still considerable. Limited computer capacity in terms of speed, memory, and screen size and resolution may make gaining access to a web survey problematic. The survey may appear different on different browsers, so it is essential to pilot the web instrument on at least the five or six most popular browsers. Instructions regarding the best choice of browser can be included in the instructions. Web surveys with too much embedded audio, video, or other visual aids may slow down the respondent's computer, leading to frustration and possible abandonment of survey completion midstream. Any other type of technical glitch encountered during survey completion may result in non-completion. In addition, the frame populations most likely to be appropriate for web surveys probably suffer from email and possibly web survey fatigue. Only the most salient surveys will be completed. Because of the online format, it is difficult to entice potential respondents with incentives, and trying to do so through attempting to get mailing addresses may actually reduce the response rate. However, it is possible to provide web-based incentives such as links to vouchers. Also, web surveys that are not protected by PIN numbers may be subject to corruption by individuals with the goal of distorting or invalidating the results.

Although surveys hosted on secure servers give the impression that anonymity is preserved and 'tend to feel safer providing honest answers in an online environment' (Sue and Ritter, 2007: 5), it is critical to be aware that laws in various countries may supersede such anonymity. For example, the US Patriot Act allows authorities to gain access to the records of internet providers. As such, survey research conducted at universities may require such a statement to be included in the cover letter of a web survey, in this example referring to the US-based web hosting company Zoomerang:

Zoomerang is an on-line survey company owned and operated by Market Tolls, Inc., located in California USA, and as such is subject to U.S. laws. In particular, the US Patriot Act which allows authorities access to the records of internet service providers. Zoomerang servers record incoming IP addresses of the computer that you use to access the survey but no connection is made between your data and your computer's IP address. If you choose to participate in the survey, you understand that your responses to the survey questions will be stored and accessed in the USA. The security and privacy policy for Zoomerang can be found at the following link: http://www.markettools.com/company/privacy-policy

---

TEXT BOX 4.1

Ethics Alert!

Laws regarding privacy, confidentiality, and anonymity may vary by country.

When conducting international comparative survey research, it is essential to investigate the laws of different countries regarding issues of privacy, confidentiality, and anonymity. Any potential breeches must be disclosed to potential respondents.

For many of the reasons cited above, response rates for web surveys continue to be low. Sensible error-free design, regular follow-ups, and elimination of confidentiality concerns will enhance response rates.

Interviewer-administered surveys

The goal of an interviewer-administered survey is to ensure that a person trained in the art, science, and technical aspects of interviewing leads the interviewee through the items on a survey instrument. This format is advantageous in that the interviewer is able to establish rapport with the interviewee, answer questions, clarify any ambiguities, ensure that all questions are answered, and ask probing questions to ensure more complete responses to open-ended questions. An interviewer-administered survey employs an aural channel of communication that can be augmented by a visual channel through the use of visual aids such as response categories (Weisberg, 2005: 32). Once interviewees have agreed to participate in an interview, often it is possible to conduct longer interviews and to ask detailed open-ended questions.

These advantages can be offset by a number of disadvantages. The presence of an interviewer can be as much of a liability as an asset. Interviewers bring with them a sense of appeal or lack thereof through their appearance, gender, race/ethnicity, age, educational level, attitudes, and other personal characteristics. The level of professionalism and skill at interviewing possessed by the interviewer will

Cartoon 4.1

Speed Bump used with the permission of Dave Coverly and the Cartoonist Group. All rights reserved.

affect the quality of the interview. Interviewers can also affect the results of the data through the use of leading questions, confirming or disaffirming behaviour (e.g., agreeing with or frowning at responses). Also, interviewees may be reluctant to share personal or sensitive information with an interviewer.

There are several general disadvantages beyond the characteristics and control of the interviewer. Interviews are resource-intensive and hence expensive. Although response rates for this format tend to be high, tracking down interviewees with busy lives and arranging for dates and times to conduct the interviews can be very time-consuming. Unless the research budget is huge, the sample size tends to be smaller.

Telephone surveys

Due to rapid technological advances in the field of telecommunications, the halcyon days of telephone interviewing appear to be over. Up until recently, telephone surveys were favoured, particularly by government and large polling agencies. However, unlisted landline numbers, an increase in mobile phone use without related telephone directories, caller IDs, and answering machines allow individuals to cocoon themselves away from unsolicited and unwanted contact. Legislation forbidding telemarketing companies from contacting individuals who have registered with their services echoes public sentiment.

The Wikipedia entry 'Do Not Call List' (http://en.wikipedia.org/wiki/Do_not_call_list) provides an up-to-date listing of countries with such legislation and related links. Exceptions (of which legitimate survey research is usually one) and loopholes related to these registries are described on the individual websites.

TEXT BOX 4.2

Do Not Call Lists

Canada *National Do Not Call List* of the Canadian Radio-television and Telecommunications Commission www.lnnte-dncl.gc.ca

UK *Telephone Preference Service (TPS)* administered by the Office of Communications http://www.tpsonline.org.uk/tps/

National Do Not Call Registry administered by the Federal Trade Commission https://www.donotcall.gov/.

Despite the coverage problems described above, telephone interviews do have some advantages above and beyond other interviewer-administered formats. Data can be collected rapidly over a short period of time, which might be critical when the purpose of the survey is to assess the mood of respondents on a time-dependent issue (e.g., views about a proposed government policy). However, in order to collect data rapidly the study would need to have a team of interviewers at its disposal as it would be beyond the ability of a single interviewer to conduct enough interviews over the course of a day or two to create a meaningfully analysable data set. Because there is no face-to-face contact, anonymity between the interviewer and interviewee may be an advantage. At the same time, the human voice of the interviewer and the interactive nature of the interview may be an asset in establishing a sense of trust and rapport with the interviewee. Telephone interviewers are able to enter responses to questions directly into the computer in real time, which hastens the data entry phase.

Telephone interviews are less expensive than face-to-face interviews. Also, they are geographically limited only by a given jurisdiction's telecommunications infrastructure. Long-distance rates for landlines have become very competitive, resulting in lower costs per interview. Long-distance costs can be reduced even further through Voice over Internet Protocol networks such as VoipStunt or Skype. Moreover, computer-to-computer calls with Skype are free. Skype has the added advantage of allowing conversations to be recorded. Other technological advances such as Dragon (PC) or Dragon Dictate (Mac) can be employed to lower costs further by digitally transcribing interview conversations containing open-ended questions. Built-in webcam features can be used to turn telephone interviews into quasi-face-to-face interviews.

There are several disadvantages to telephone interviews. Although anonymity may be an asset, the interviewee may doubt the credibility of an interviewer whose legitimacy cannot be verified. As such, interviewees may be reluctant to provide personal information such as income level to a faceless questioner. Unless prearranged, telephone interviews are disruptive and if they extend beyond 20–30 minutes, interviewees may simply hang up. Hence, it is important at the beginning of the interview to specify accurately how long the interview will take. A long series of questions with related multiple categories can be tedious to listen to and may lead to less precise responses. Telephone interviewees are more likely to answer nearer to the pole of each response category. Also, it is not possible to use visual aids unless they can be sent in advance. Survey instruments must be designed specifically for the telephone. In particular, length and formatting must suit the format.

Face-to-face interviews

Face-to-face interviews entail a physical encounter between an interviewer and interviewee. Such interviews can be employed with a variety of samples, such as random sampling, intercept or exit polls, or the special case of snowball sampling when gaining access to respondents who would otherwise be unreachable (e.g., the homeless) by any other means would be difficult or impossible. Beyond the general advantages of interviewer-administered surveys, face-to-face interviews have numerous advantages. The interviewer is not faceless; hence, her/his legitimacy can be demonstrated through official credentials and a professional demeanour. Because interviewers are physically present, they can use visual aids, ask probing questions, and act on visual cues such as a puzzled expression on the face of the interviewee. Other formats, such as a pen-and-paper or computer survey, can also be employed during a face-to-face interview when, for example, sensitive questions are posed. Also, semi-structured open-ended questions can be posed as well as open-ended questions that may arise during the course of the interview (e.g., picking up on a topic that was not directly in line with the structured part of the survey; acting on contextual cues of the interviewee's home, dress, appearance, presence of family members, to name a few), adding flexibility. The ability of interviewer to enter data directly in a computer during the interview is often cited as an advantage; however, in terms of engaging with the interviewee this practice could be a distraction and may be considered rude.

As with all formats, face-to-face interviews have several disadvantages. They are expensive in terms of both time and money to conduct. When the geographic territory is large, interviewer-administered surveys are difficult to carry out because of the time and travel costs. As a result, they tend to be constrained to specific geographic areas. Because this format involves face-to-face contact – that is, no anonymity – and often audio recording of the interview, interviewees may be more anxious and less able to communicate effectively. The interaction of gender, appearance, race/ethnicity, and the persona of both the interviewer and interviewee may affect the quality of the interview. In addition, safety concerns for the interviewer must be kept in mind, especially when interviews are conducted in homes or with hard-to-reach populations. The training of interviewers is discussed in Chapter 8.

Mixing modes and methods

In this chapter, I have presented each format in its pure form. However, some formats can easily be combined with other formats with the goal of enhancing their effectiveness. As already noted, pen-and-paper surveys can be administered to interviewees partaking in a face-to-face interview. Here I return to the discussion on mixed modes and mixed methods introduced at the beginning of the chapter.

Mixed modes

Any of the formats described above can be combined to enhance response rates. When doing so, the idea of a unimode construction of each instrument developed for a given format should be considered seriously. For example, if telephone and survey formats are employed in a study, the instruments should be adapted to be as compatible as possible. Doing so will involve compromises that will, on the one hand, ensure more comparability of the data and, on the other hand, diminish the effectiveness of one of the formats. For example, it is likely to be necessary to reduce the complexity of the instrument used in the face-to-face interviews to be in line with the telephone component. It is important to be vigilant in what is being gained and lost in a unimode approach.

A mixed mode approach can also be employed within a given format. For example, when arranging dates and times for a telephone interview, potential interviewees could be contacted initially by telephone. Those who are unreachable by telephone could be contacted by email or mail (if email, mailing addresses, or both are known). de Leeuw and Hox (2008) provide good examples of types of mixed mode designs. Again, the goal in a *unimode* approach is to ensure that the modes of contact are as parallel as possible.

Mixed methods

From a mixed methods perspective, any of the formats above may also be combined. However, the goal is not to enhance response rates, but rather to enrich the quality of the data collected by employing two or more formats that can tap into the strengths of each format. A typical combination is to conduct mail surveys with a larger sample of, for example, all employees of a company, followed by face-to-face interviews with a smaller subset of those who responded to the mail survey. In this example, the goals of the two formats are not the same. The mail survey component is used to collect data in which broad patterns can be established. Face-to-face interviews are conducted, for example, to allow interviewees to provide more detailed answers to the questions posed on the mail survey or to be invited to explain some of the findings (see Cresswell et al., 2008, for a detailed discussion of different mixed methods designs). The goal is to create a data set with complementary and competing findings in order to determine convergence, inconsistency, and contradiction (Mathison, 1988) among the findings.

In addition, a mixed methods approach can be employed within a given format. For example, once a sampling frame is determined, individuals may be first approached through an email invitation. In this letter of invitation, respondents are invited to participate in a web survey. Those who do not complete the surveys within a given period of time may be contacted by telephone. Ultimately, persistent non-participants may be sent a letter in the mail encouraging them to complete the web survey. The difference in this approach from that of a unimode approach is subtle. In this mixed methods example, the goal is to use the best method at each step of the survey process. This example reminds us yet again that survey research is naturally amenable to a mixed methods design.

Mixed methods designs are more demanding in terms of time, resources, and the skill sets of the researchers. Such studies may take more time to complete as, by design, they involve more than one format. It may be necessary for researchers to work in teams to ensure that they have the skills required to complete a study.

Summary

This chapter began with a discussion of mixed mode versus mixed methods survey research designs. A discussion of self-administered and interviewer-administered formats followed. Under self-administered formats, the modes of group administered surveys, mail surveys, email surveys and web surveys were described.

Telephone and face-to-face surveys were explained under the heading of interviewer-administered surveys. At the end of the chapter, mixed mode and mixed methods survey research designs were revisited in light of the different survey formats.

Exercises

1 Begin to plan the development of the survey instrument(s) to be used in your survey project. Consider which approach(es) would be most appropriate for your research questions: group survey, mail-out survey, telephone survey, face-to-face survey, email survey, or web survey.

2 Write down the advantages and disadvantages of each format.

3 Consider the possibility of employing a mixed mode approach, a mixed methods approach, or both. What are the strengths and weaknesses of employing one or both of these approaches?

Further reading

Bergman, M. M. (ed.) (2008). *Advances in Mixed Methods Research.* London: Sage.
Dillman, D. A. (2000). *Mail and Internet Surveys. The Tailored Design Method.* New York: Wiley.

FIVE

Developing survey questions

Cartoon 5.1

By permission of John L. Hart FLP and Creators Syndicate, Inc.

Having worked through the development of concepts, constructs, and indicator variables, as described in Chapter 3, you are now well positioned to develop survey items. It cannot be stressed enough that survey items must be designed with extreme care. As little as a misplaced or carelessly chosen word can alter the meaning of a question and may render it ultimately unusable or uninterpretable.

In this chapter, the minutiae of survey questionnaire construction are presented. Through the use of numerous examples, I describe how to word questions clearly in order to elicit the intended response, and present the various types of measurement and scale construction formats. I emphasize the advantages of using multiple indicators to create latent constructs – from both quantitative and qualitative perspectives. The use of closed- and open-ended questions is encouraged. Also, I discuss the value of enhancing the appearance of written and online forms of surveys through the use of illustration and graphic design. Finally, I stress the importance of piloting survey instruments.

Designing survey questions

The opening words of Stanley Payne's (1951: 3) infamous book on questionnaire design are as follows: 'Why concern yourself? A plea for the importance of asking good questions'. He and others argue, quite correctly, that many survey methods books place too little emphasis on the design of survey items and instead direct the majority of attention to sampling issues. As he so wisely pointed out, 'improvements in question wording and in other phases can contribute far more to the accuracy than further improvements in sampling methods can'; he then advises that rather than 'trying to knock a few more tenths of a percent off the statistical error', survey samplers' efforts could be better directed at trying to eliminate the 'tens of percents' (p. 5) lost through poor survey wording.

Survey items range from closed dichotomous questions (Example 5.1) at one extreme to completely open-ended questions (Example 5.2) at the other.

Example 5.1   Closed dichotomous question

Are you: (Check **one**)

female ..☐$_1$

male .....☐$_0$

Example 5.2   Completely open-ended question

Do you have any final comments or thoughts that you want to share with us?

Comments:

_____

_____

_____

_____

_____

_____

In between these two extremes, there are a myriad of ways to ask questions. Designing questionnaires can be daunting. However, as Nussbaum (2002: 135) points out, '[a]nything worth measuring in human quality of life, is difficult to measure'. In the course of completing a survey, most of us have been frustrated by questions and related response categories that did not correspond with our experiences, attitudes, behaviours, or even our demographic characteristics. A good questionnaire often requires that questions be designed with multiple lenses aimed at the same construct. This may require that a series of questions are employed, that several questions are asked from slightly different perspectives, or that closed-ended questions are combined with open-ended questions to ensure that respondents are able to provide full and accurate responses to questions.

But how does one begin? Below, I provide some rules of thumb to get you started on the road to designing your survey.

Rules of thumb for getting started

Brainstorm ideas

A logical place to start is with your research questions. These questions will have been specified through the process of identifying the key constructs for your study. By now, you will have formulated, at least in a rough sense, questions corresponding to your research questions. These initial formulations can be further developed by brainstorming ideas for questionnaire items based on all the work you did to conceptualize your study. These ideas should be written down under the corresponding research question.

At this stage it is important to ensure that each of your ideas for survey items fit under each of your research questions. If these ideas fall outside of your research questions, you must make a decision: (1) to eliminate such questions as they are extraneous to your study; or (2) add one or more additional research questions to accommodate such survey items. Otherwise, the survey may become unfocused and unwieldy.

Use existing questions

In some instances, it is highly advisable to use existing questions. For example, questions designed to measure occupational status on national censuses have undergone extensive testing. Also, occupational coding schemes, and often related occupational prestige scales, have been devised to correspond to such survey items. This collection of tools related to a survey question is invaluable in comparing your research with studies employing either census data or other studies using the same measures. Also, available coding schemes allow for the data to be reduced in standardized ways.

For example, in Canada, on the long form of the Census (Example 5.3), a series of questions about occupational status is posed. Answers to this question can be coded using the Canadian National Occupational Classification (http://www5.hrsdc.gc.ca/noc/english/noc/2006/QuickSearch.aspx?val65=*). Similar classification schemes are available for many countries, including the United States (http://www.bls.gov/soc/), the United Kingdom (http://www.ons.gov.uk/about-statistics/classifications/archived/SOC2000/index.html), and Australia (http://www.abs.gov.au/ausstats/abs@.nsf/0/A630E3FD6A69F7CCCA25697E001851DA?opendocument).

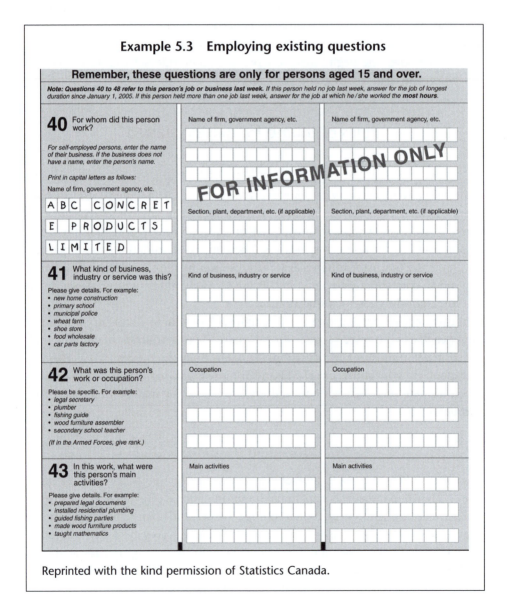

Example 5.3   Employing existing questions

Reprinted with the kind permission of Statistics Canada.

Other standardized questions that may be useful to incorporate into your survey include those measuring race/ethnicity or levels of educational attainment. However, these questions should not be adopted blindly. It is essential to determine whether they are good indicators of the construct you are trying to measure. Also, even standardized questions need to be pilot-tested with individuals similar to your intended respondents. Words such as 'minority' or 'ethnicity' may not be understandable to, say, high school students.

Existing questions and plagiarism

It is a commonly held view that borrowing questions from other surveys is an acceptable practice. Technically, however, this practice falls under the definition of plagiarism. According to the American Psychological Association (2010: 170):

> Reproduce word for word material directly quoted from another author's work or from your own previously published work, material duplicated from a test item, and verbatim instructions to participants. ... If the short quotation comprises fewer than 40 words, incorporate it into the text and enclose the quotation with double quotation marks.

It would be impractical and distracting to present survey items in quotes. However, as an ethical researcher, you must ensure whether permission, credit, or both is required on borrowed survey items. Post-secondary academic discipline committees take issues of plagiarism very seriously. If you are working within a post-secondary setting, it is imperative to read the institution's policy on academic integrity.

TEXT BOX 5.1

Ethics Alert!

When borrowing questions from others' surveys, ensure that you are not conducting an act of plagiarism.

Also, you and your research supervisor may want to consult with staff who are responsible for academic integrity issues to determine how to cite the original sources of your survey items. Permission to use copyrighted items must be obtained. Often, there are fees associated with using copyrighted items.

Use existing questions as a starting point

In the process of conducting an extensive literature review, you may have examined surveys used to collect data on a topic similar to your own. However, because

---

the context, sample, and temporal framework are unique to your study, previous surveys and related questions may often serve, at best, as a guide. It is useful to examine the way in which other questions have been asked, the type of question that was used – that is, whether an open- or closed-ended question was employed, and if the latter, what type of scale was employed. Existing questions may be modified into a form suitable for your study, or may serve as a source of inspiration for a new question.

Guiding principles for questionnaire item design

Before beginning to create survey items, the following four principles must be kept in mind. These are 'guiding principles' in that they should be considered as the general rule. Because there is no 'one size fits all' formula for questionnaire design, exceptions to these principles may be legitimate. However, it is worth the effort to evaluate each of your questions in relation to these principles in order to determine whether it is wise to violate them.

1 *Ask questions that your respondents can actually answer* and that produce meaningful results. Respondents must have knowledge, experience, and insights specific

"HOW MANY KIDS WE GOT NOW, DORIS ?"

Cartoon 5.2

Reprinted with permission of www.CartoonStock.com. All rights reserved.

DESIGNING AND DOING SURVEY RESEARCH

to your research questions in order to be useful informants. In turn, survey questions need to tap into the knowledge, experience, and insights of respondents. Example 5.4 illustrates a question that (1) cannot be answered in any meaningful way, and (2) cannot produce meaningful results.

Example 5.4   An ambiguous question

What is your current primary goal in life? (Check **only one** response)

    a. family/home responsibilities ......$\square_1$

    b. my career ....$\square_2$

    c. my education ....$\square_3$

    d. something else ....$\square_4$

    e. a combination of things ....$\square_5$

Survey questions, for the most part, are limited to those about *behaviours, attitudes, perceptions, beliefs, facts,* and *demographic characteristics* of the respondent. Asking respondents about the traits of, for example, their family members or co-workers requires an exercise of speculation which may not result in very accurate information.

2 *Ensure that each question includes only one thought or idea.* This includes both the stem of the questionnaire and the response categories. 'Double-barrelled questions', that is, those containing more than one thought or idea, are discussed later in this chapter. Such questions confuse the respondent and are impossible to analyse. The question in Example 5.5 contains several thoughts, including 'comments or behaviours', 'race, place of origin, ancestry, or skin colour', and 'academic or work performance'.

Example 5.5   A double-barrelled question

During this past year, did you experience any unwanted and unwelcome comments or behaviours concerning your race, place of origin, ancestry, or skin colour that had a negative impact on your academic or work performance?

    Yes ....$\square_1$

    No ....$\square_0$

A respondent may have one view about unwelcome comments about her/his race that impacted work performance, and quite another on the impact of unwanted comments about her/his place of origin on academic performance. The wording of this question prohibits the teasing out of discrete ideas and, as such, is not very useful in understanding these relationships.

3 *Choose your words carefully.* Use plain, simple, and clear language when possible. Avoid technical terms for a non-technical audience (this principle may be violated for highly specialized groups who share a common technical language). Sixty years ago, Payne (1951) developed '1000 frequent-familiar words' for the English language which are still useful as a guideline for choosing words. Even this list is complex in that it contains both 'problem words' and 'multi-meaning words' (p. 151).

4 *Provide instructions on how to answer the question.* For example, it may be necessary to include one or more of the following types of instructions: (1) whether one or more than one response is required; (2) the temporal period in which the response should be framed; (3) definitions of terms that may not have clear meanings; and (4) skip instructions. Each of these details is taken up again later in the chapter.

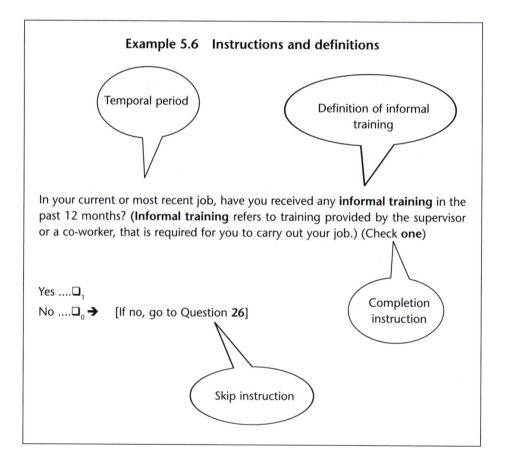

Example 5.6 Instructions and definitions

Now we are ready to move on to the types of questions that can be used in our surveys. Initially, I will present types of questions that can be used for any type of survey format (i.e., self-administered versus interviewer-administered). At the end of the chapter, I will discuss the peculiarities of questionnaire design in relation to survey format.

Types of questions

At the beginning of this chapter, I highlighted the two extremes of question types. From a mixed methods perspective, it is impossible to privilege one type of questionnaire format over the other or to separate them into two camps. Research, especially survey research, is costly and time-consuming, so every question we pose must be done in a way to maximize the information obtained to answer our research questions. In this section, I work through the various types of question styles that can be used to gather information through surveys. Although I begin this section with closed dichotomous questions, immediately I demonstrate how the addition of other elements, including additional categories or open-ended questions, can greatly expand the depth of information and maximize the quality of responses provided. Although many books distinguish between questions measuring knowledge and questions measuring attitudes (e.g., Sudman and Bradburn, 1982), the principles and techniques for creating all types of questions is the same. Hence, I do not make such distinctions.

Two-way or dichotomous closed-ended questions as starting points

A two-way or dichotomous question is the most closed of closed-ended questions in that it divides responses, and hence respondents, into two categories. These categories can be dichotomies such as 'yes/no', 'better/worse', 'male/female'. The advantages and disadvantages of this type of question are the same: specificity and simplicity. For some questions such as biological sex (Example 5.1 above), in most instances, the specific and simple dichotomous 'male/female' response categories are precisely what is needed.

However, between the categories of 'black' and 'white' contain a 'rainbow' of behaviours, attitudes, preferences, and lived experiences of individuals. A dichotomous question may be efficient, but not very effective for capturing the information that we seek.

Completely open-ended questions

Open-ended questions allow the respondent to provide answers in the form of words – either written or spoken – to a question. Example 5.2 is an example of a completely open-ended question. Completely open-ended questions have several advantages. They provide the respondent with the opportunity to comment or expand upon the other questions in the survey. Because responses are unstructured, respondents may raise issues that had not been considered by the researchers but are nevertheless important. Responses to open-ended questions can be used to inform subsequent development of survey questions. In addition, sensitive issues or topics addressing 'disapproved' behaviour, such as substance abuse, may be better approached through an open-ended question format (Bradburn and Sudman, 1979; Converse and Presser, 1986; Weisberg, 2005).

Transcribing, coding and analysing completely open-ended questions is more challenging than with closed-ended questions. However, with the availability of advanced qualitative analysis software such as ATLAS.ti and voice recognition software such as Dragon and Dragon Dictate, this task is vastly easier to carry out.

Like two-way or dichotomous closed-ended questions, the spectrum of the rainbow of completely open-ended questions can be concentrated. Open-ended questions can follow closed-ended questions, or they can be written in a way to focus the desired responses. In the next section, I demonstrate how to expand two-way or dichotomous closed-ended questions to be more inclusive.

Other types of closed-ended questions

Middle-ground categories

Closed-ended questions can be expanded by adding more response categories. One way of doing this is to add a 'middle-ground' category, that is, one that is between two extremes such as 'yes' and 'no' in Example 5.6. While forcing a respondent to answer in one of the two extremes may be efficient and provide tidy information, it may not be accurate. As Payne (1951: 62) indicates, 'an intermediate position is also a definite possibility'. Example 5.7 is such a question which is supported by the literature.

Example 5.7   Dichotomous questions with a middle-ground category

If you do not have children, do you think you might begin starting a family within the next 3 years?

No ....☐$_1$

Maybe ....☐$_2$

Yes ....☐$_3$

Closed-ended dichotomous question followed by an open-ended question

Another way of expanding responses to a question is to use a closed-ended dichotomous question followed by an open-ended question (Example 5.8). This approach has two distinct advantages. First, it provides respondents with the opportunity to explain their answers. Second, it could lead eventually to the development of new questions on the topic.

Example 5.8   Closed-ended question with an open-ended response component

If you could choose again, would you make the same educational choices? (Check **one**)

No ......☐$_0$

Yes ......☐$_1$

Please use the space below to explain your answer.

_____

_____

Questions can be expanded by adding several categories. One way of doing this is by creating unordered response categories.

Unordered response categories

In this type of question, a stem is followed by a number of unordered response categories that are related to each other. For example, a global stem question about employer-provided benefits (Example 5.9) is followed by several discrete response categories. Respondents are instructed to answer each response category individually.

Example 5.9   Unordered response question

Does your current or most recent employer provide you with the following?
(Check **one for each line**)

	Yes	No
A pension plan?	$\square_1$	$\square_0$
Medical insurance?	$\square_1$	$\square_0$
A dental plan?	$\square_1$	$\square_0$
Paid parental leave?	$\square_1$	$\square_0$
Child-care benefits?	$\square_1$	$\square_0$
Sick leave?	$\square_1$	$\square_0$
Long term disability?	$\square_1$	$\square_0$
Life insurance?	$\square_1$	$\square_0$
Leave for personal reasons?	$\square_1$	$\square_0$
Retirement planning programs?	$\square_1$	$\square_0$
Other (specify) _____	$\square_1$	$\square_0$

The unordered response category format is necessary for questions on topics such as religion, race/ethnicity or other nominal variables.

Ordered response categories

Of course, questions can be expanded beyond two extremes and possibly a third middle-ground category. One way to do so is to add ordered response categories in the form of a rating scale. As Payne (1951: 70) states, 'a "good" two-way question will have only two possible sides if we disregard the middle-ground and no-opinion replies. If any other stand is possible, then either the issue is not clear or it just is not a two-way issue'.

Rating scales

Rating scales are anchored in two extremes with several anchor points in between. Common extremes are 'very good' to 'very poor', 'definitely false' to 'definitely true',' and 'never' to 'always'. Rating scales usually offer at least four categories. This structure can be used for a single question (Example 5.10), or it can be used to ask a series of questions under an umbrella stem (Example 5.11).

Example 5.10 Rating scales

How often do you participate in regular exercise (e.g., running, football, walking, weight training, yoga)?

Not at all ....$\square_1$

Once a week ....$\square_2$

Two to three times a week ....$\square_3$

Four to five times a week ....$\square_4$

More than five times a week ....$\square_5$

Example 5.11 A single rating scale for multiple questions

When choosing a spouse or partner, to what extent do you believe it is important that both people share the following qualities? (Check **one for each line**)

	Extent of importance:				
	Not at all important	Not very important	Neither important nor unimportant	Some what important	Very important
a. Similar educational background	$\square_1$	$\square_2$	$\square_3$	$\square_4$	$\square_5$
b. Similar moral values	$\square_1$	$\square_2$	$\square_3$	$\square_4$	$\square_5$
c. Similar political views	$\square_1$	$\square_2$	$\square_3$	$\square_4$	$\square_5$
d. Similar ethnic background	$\square_1$	$\square_2$	$\square_3$	$\square_4$	$\square_5$
e. Same racial group	$\square_1$	$\square_2$	$\square_3$	$\square_4$	$\square_5$
f. Similar attitudes toward work	$\square_1$	$\square_2$	$\square_3$	$\square_4$	$\square_5$
g. Similar religion	$\square_1$	$\square_2$	$\square_3$	$\square_4$	$\square_5$
h. Similar sense of humour	$\square_1$	$\square_2$	$\square_3$	$\square_4$	$\square_5$
i. Similar social class (e.g., economic background/income)	$\square_1$	$\square_2$	$\square_3$	$\square_4$	$\square_5$
j. Similar views about parenting	$\square_1$	$\square_2$	$\square_3$	$\square_4$	$\square_5$

A good rating scale consists of the following features. First, it is balanced; that is, the categories should be constructed so that there are equal proportions of anchor points on each side of the scale. Second, each anchor point is labelled, so that all respondent are interpreting the scale in the same way. In doing so, 'all of the points are more consistently calibrated by the use of words' (Fowler, 1995: 53). Third, there is consensus that scales should contain no more than seven categories, but five is probably sufficient. Providing labels for more than five anchor points can be problematic. The mode of survey delivery will be an important consideration in the number of categories included on the survey instrument (Fowler, 1995: 53; Weisberg, 2005). This issue is taken up later in this chapter.

Midpoints on rating scales

In Example 5.11 above, a midpoint is included in the scale. There is considerable debate in the literature about the virtues and perils of including a midpoint in scales. As with the 'yes/no' format, some people may hold views that fall between these two extremes. If there is no midpoint, individuals are not allowed to sit on the fence. Research has demonstrated that individuals respond differently to questions with and without midpoints on scales. For example, Converse and Presser (1986) report that, when offered as a category, up to 20% of respondents will choose a middle category.

How to decide? Detailed knowledge of your sample should help guide you in deciding whether to construct scales that force your respondents to choose one side of the fence or to allow them to choose a midpoint. In addition, the nature of the question may influence the scale that you employ. Also, the ethics and the value of forced choice responses should be considered.

TEXT BOX 5.2

Ethics Alert!

Consider the ethical implications of forcing individuals to choose, or offering them an opportunity to sit on the fence.

Neutral, no opinion, not applicable

Whereas midpoints belong logically on a continuum, categories such as 'neutral', 'no opinion', 'undecided', or 'not applicable' fall outside the continuum.

These categories are legitimate options and should be offered, when appropriate. Otherwise, answers provided by those without opinions due to lack of knowledge or interest may be unstable (Sudman and Bradburn, 1982). However, as Stern et al. (2007) demonstrate, their position in a scale can affect the results. Such options should be positioned outside the rating scale (Dillman, 2000). In Example 5.12, the options 'no opinion' and 'not applicable' are included but are located outside the continuum of response choices.

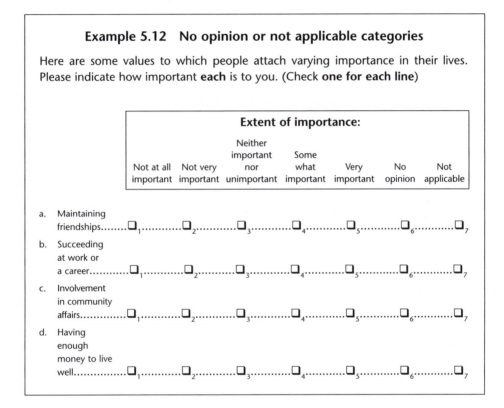

Example 5.12   No opinion or not applicable categories

Here are some values to which people attach varying importance in their lives. Please indicate how important **each** is to you. (Check **one for each line**)

Another way to approach those without opinions or for whom the question is not applicable is to begin with a filtering or screening question (Converse and Presser, 1986; Fowler, 1995: 76).

On a scale of 1 to 10

Because a scale of '1 to 10' is used commonly in everyday language, it is familiar to most people. It is useful for questions such as those addressing happiness and well-being (Example 5.13). It is not necessary to label each point.

Example 5.13   Scale of 1 to 10 question

On a scale of **1** to **10**, in general how happy would you say you are with your life? (Circle **one**)

Very									Very
unhappy									happy

1..........2..........3..........4..........5..........6..........7..........8..........9..........10

Ranking scales

In questions employing a ranking scale, respondents are asked to order the response categories from 'most' to 'least' in some way. In Example 5.14, respondents are asked to rank, from 'most important' to 'least important', factors they consider when choosing to frequent a restaurant or pub.

Example 5.14   Ranking scale

Please rank order the following items from most important to least, when you are choosing a health food store.

(1 = most important, 8 = least important. Please rank each item once only)

	1	2	3	4	5	6	7	8
Price of merchandise	$\square_1$	$\square_2$	$\square_3$	$\square_4$	$\square_5$	$\square_6$	$\square_7$	$\square_8$
Range of organic food	$\square_1$	$\square_2$	$\square_3$	$\square_4$	$\square_5$	$\square_6$	$\square_7$	$\square_8$
Uniqueness of products	$\square_1$	$\square_2$	$\square_3$	$\square_4$	$\square_5$	$\square_6$	$\square_7$	$\square_8$
Variety of vegetarian products	$\square_1$	$\square_2$	$\square_3$	$\square_4$	$\square_5$	$\square_6$	$\square_7$	$\square_8$
Friendliness of staff	$\square_1$	$\square_2$	$\square_3$	$\square_4$	$\square_5$	$\square_6$	$\square_7$	$\square_8$
Atmosphere	$\square_1$	$\square_2$	$\square_3$	$\square_4$	$\square_5$	$\square_6$	$\square_7$	$\square_8$
Location	$\square_1$	$\square_2$	$\square_3$	$\square_4$	$\square_5$	$\square_6$	$\square_7$	$\square_8$
Community relations	$\square_1$	$\square_2$	$\square_3$	$\square_4$	$\square_5$	$\square_6$	$\square_7$	$\square_8$

Ranking questions are difficult to complete and often result in respondent frustration (Krosnick, 1999). Questions that require all items in a long list to be ranked are particularly challenging, as individuals may not hold strong views beyond one or two items. Example 5.14 was an online survey question. It was impossible to move on to the next question until all items were ranked. In addition, respondents may choose to assign equal ranks to response categories, which makes analysis difficult. Unlike rating scales that specify calibrations between categories, there is no way to assess different distances between ranks. In addition, ranking scales are methodologically problematic. The rank of one item is not independent of the other items 'since the prior ranking determines the relative ranks of the remaining ones' (Hino and Imai, 2008: 2). This leads to a negative correlation bias. Although questions using rating scales are susceptible to positive response set biases, responses to each question are independent, and hence preferable. Also, in practice, questions using rating scales are easier to answer.

Fill in the blanks

Sometimes, just asking respondents to fill in one or more blanks may be the most effective way of posing the question. When possible, it is desirable to collect continuous data – that is, data that appear on a continuum with intervals that are of equal distance (Example 5.15). Statistical techniques allow us to aggregate up, but it is not possible to disaggregate categorical data down. Unless there is good reason to provide categories (e.g., age ranges, broad categories for education levels), try to collect information in the most disaggregated form possible.

Example 5.15 Fill in the blanks

What is your birth date?   _____   _____   _____

year   month   day

Aggregation can happen at the level of analysis. Analysis is often iterative. Once you have collected the data you will see what else you can investigate. You may regret not having asked a question in the level of detail that you might want at a later date.

Asking a series of questions

Sometimes, it is necessary to ask a series of questions to arrive at the response you are trying to obtain. In Example 5.16, while some of the response categories make sense, others do not. For example, a negative response to the item 'moved out of the family home' could mean that the respondent (1) still lives in the family home or (2) did not live in the family home in the first place, and hence did not move out. Also 'family home' may mean one's parents' home or perhaps one's own home in the case of a divorce or separation. In Example 5.17, a series of questions are employed to ask about the same topic – returning to the parental home.

Example 5.16   An ambiguous question

Between January 1, 2011 and December 31, 2011, have you done any of the following? (Check all that apply)

a. completed your studies...................$\square_1$

b. moved out of the family home.......$\square_2$

c. entered the labour force.................$\square_3$

d. took out a mortgage.....................$\square_4$

e. got married.................................$\square_5$

f. started a family...........................$\square_6$

Additional issues in questionnaire design

Choosing a question format is an important step in questionnaire design. However, there are also several other issues to consider. As Payne (1951: 72) points out, ' a "good" question, among other things, is one which does not affect the answer'. In the following section, I will address several issues that may affect the responses to survey items.

Stems and response categories with multiple dimensions

As little as one word can distort the meaning of a question and render it unusable. In Example 5.18, the use of 'sometimes' in the stem conflicts with the 'strongly disagree' to 'strongly agree' scale. Question stems and response categories must be scrutinized for conflicting dimensions. Similarly, respondents will be confused by questions containing double negatives or double superlatives.

Example 5.17   A series of questions

1.a.   Who currently lives in your household? (Check **all that apply**)

I am living alone..................................$\square_1$

My female spouse/partner.....................$\square_2$

My male spouse/partner.......................$\square_3$

One or more children...........................$\square_4$

One or both parents.............................$\square_5$

Brother or sister..................................$\square_6$

In-laws..$\square_7$

Roommate or friends...........................$\square_8$

Other relatives....................................$\square_9$

1.b.   Since **September 2005**, have you returned to live with your parents/guardians? (Check **one**)

No.........$\square_0$ ➜   [If no, go to Question 3, **next page**]

Yes.........$\square_1$

1.c.   In what year since **September 2005** did you last return to live there?

Year: _____

1.d.   Why did you return to live there?

_____

_____

_____

2.a.   Are you still living with your parents/guardians? (Check **one**)

No.........$\square_0$ ➜   [If no, go to Question **5**, **next page**]

Yes.........$\square_1$

2.b.   If yes, why have you made the decision to continue living with your parents/ guardians?

_____

_____

_____

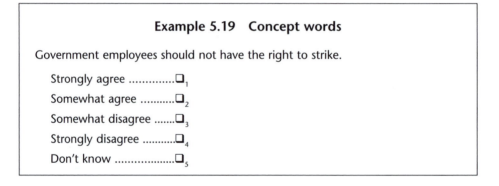

Example 5.18   An ambiguous question

	Extent of agreement:			
Strongly disagree	Disagree	Neither agree nor disagree	Agree	Strongly agree

a. Sometimes, I believe that I can't get ahead without post-secondary education.........☐$_1$............☐$_2$.............☐$_3$...........☐$_4$........ ...☐$_5$

Concept words and plastic words

In Chapter 3 we worked through how to get from concepts to measurable indicators. During survey item construction, it is imperative not to let words representing concepts slip back in. Example 5.19 contains the concept words 'government' and 'employees'. Word such as these are vague because they mean different things to different people.

Example 5.19   Concept words

Government employees should not have the right to strike.

Strongly agree ....☐$_1$

Somewhat agree ....☐$_2$

Somewhat disagree ....☐$_3$

Strongly disagree ....☐$_4$

Don't know ....☐$_5$

In the same vein, Poerksen (1995) describes words such 'development' as *plastic* in that they are 'countless diffuse expressions [that] are squeezed into one concept and fastened onto one name, and this name gains a certain independence' (p. 20).

Temporal considerations

The timing of events, behaviours, and attitudes is an important dimension of survey research. Whereas some survey questions refer to the present, others refer to the past. Questions requiring individuals to recall the past need to be 'bounded'

(Converse and Presser, 1986: 20) so that the same time frame is used for all individuals. If they are not, a phenomenon called 'telescoping' occurs: events, behaviours, and attitudes are attributed to the wrong time period. With forward telescoping, events from the past are attributed to the time frame included in the question. As such, events, behaviours, and attitudes are over-reported. Backward telescoping results in under-reporting in that events, behaviours, and attitudes are removed from the time period specified in the question (Converse and Presser, 1986; Sudman and Bradburn, 1982).

Converse and Presser (1986) provide several suggestions to eliminate or reduce the effect of telescoping. First, the reference period should be reduced to as *narrow a frame* as possible. That is, instead of asking about events occurring in the last year, the reference can be narrowed to the last month or the last week. Second, the time frame can be bounded within an *average* or *typical* day or week. Third, *landmark events* such as the 2011 earthquake in Japan or the start of the school year can be used as a reference point. Finally, *memory cues* such as references to specific events can be employed.

Whether and which techniques are employed depend on the sample and the nature of the question. And, as Payne (1951: 29) reminds us, 'recall may differ from fact, and therefore, should not be taken as fact'.

Hypothetical or speculative questions

It is common wisdom that individuals are not very good at answering hypothetical or speculative questions about themselves and others. Such questions should be avoided.

Vague adjectives

Words such as 'normally' and 'regularly' are imprecise and serve to obfuscate, rather than clarify, the meaning of a question.

Double-barrelled questions

In Example 5.5, I provided an example of a double-barrelled question. Double-barrelled questions include two or more ideas or thoughts in the stem, response category, or both. Sudman and Bradburn (1982) point out the existence of the more subtle 'one-and-a-half-barrel' question. In this version, a continuum of a single dimension is disrupted by the insertion of an additional dimension. As a result, the meaning of the question is distorted and possibly hijacked.

Exercises in mathematics

Questionnaire items should be easy to complete. Occasionally, minor computations may be required, but they should be kept to a bare minimum. Example 5.20 involves calculating the costs of university study. In this example, the calculation of proportions is combined with a hypothetical question. Such a question is extremely difficult, if not impossible, to answer. A good question should not ask respondents to calculate proportions or carry out any mathematical exercise other than of the most basic nature.

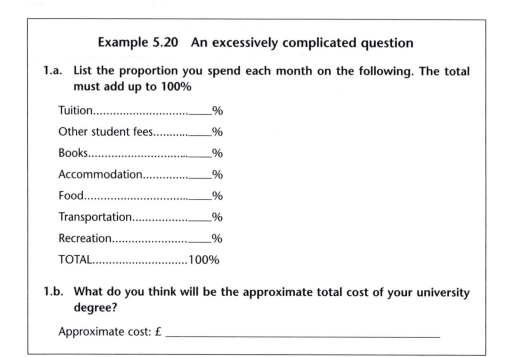

Example 5.20   An excessively complicated question

1.a.   **List the proportion you spend each month on the following. The total must add up to 100%**

Tuition.............................____%

Other student fees...........____%

Books...............................____%

Accommodation................____%

Food.................................____%

Transportation...................____%

Recreation........................____%

TOTAL.............................100%

1.b.   **What do you think will be the approximate total cost of your university degree?**

Approximate cost: £ _____

Loaded questions

Lazarsfeld and Oberschall used two real examples (shown in Example 5.21) to illustrate the use of loaded questions. The author of the first question? Max Weber. The second question? Karl Marx. Loaded questions are intended to distort responses in order to support the researcher's point of view. They are used frequently in what Weisberg (2005: 35) refers to as 'sugging' – 'selling under the guise of a survey' – and 'fugging' – 'fundraising under the guise of a survey'. Such questions have no place in legitimate research.

Example 5.21   Loaded questions

1   What depresses you most, the low level of pay, or that you are so dependent upon the employer, that you have such limited prospects to advance in life, that you have nothing to offer to your children?

2   In case of accident, is the employer obligated by law to pay compensation to the worker or his family? If not, has he ever paid compensation to those who have met with an accident while working to enrich him?

Quoted from Lazarsfeld and Oberschall (1965: 190).

Marathon questions

Like loaded questions, marathon questions are often associated with 'sugging' and 'fugging'. Example 5.22 is taken from a questionnaire by a world renowned environmentalist group. While the stem is intended to bias respondents, it also manages to exhaust them.

Example 5.22   A marathon question

Hundreds of thousands of dolphins have been killed by tuna fishermen who set their nets around dolphins to catch the tuna swimming below. Thanks to the efforts of Greenpeace and others, several large tuna companies have now promised to stop selling tuna caught at the expense of dolphins' lives. Would you support federal legislation that would require the labelling of all canned tuna products that were caught by methods that are known to kill dolphins?

❏   Yes   ❏   No   ❏   Undecided

(Greenpeace Survey, no date)

Loaded words

Individual words can also be loaded. Unlike plastic words, loaded words are intended to provoke strong emotions. The words 'depresses' and 'enrich' in Example 5.21 above illustrates how words can influence the way questions are answered.

Manipulating questions to get the answers you want

The addition of one or more response categories can change the outcome of a question. To give a real example, the addition of the single word 'the' to one of the response categories posed to voters in the referendum regarding the renaming of the Canadian cities of Fort William and Port Arthur resulted in the new amalgamated city name of Thunder Bay. The response categories were as shown in Example 5.23. The split in votes between 'Lakehead' and 'The Lakehead', meant that 'Thunder Bay' came out on top.

Example 5.23 Manipulating the answers to a survey question

a. Lakehead

b. The Lakehead

c. Thunder Bay

Sensitive topics

Often, survey items pose questions that may be considered sensitive or too personal. Questions about income, sexual behaviour, drug and alcohol use are examples of sensitive topics. Such questions may simply not be answered by respondents, or they may provide inaccurate responses which often lean toward more social acceptability.

There are several ways to pose questions on sensitive topics to improve both the response rates and the accuracy of responses. First, providing assurances of the anonymity of responses is critical. On a self-administered survey, assurances can be included in the cover letter and in the stem of individual questions, as in Example 5.24.

Example 5.24   Sensitive topics

Have you ever had a student loan? (Check **one**)

(Please remember that all information provided on this survey will be reported anonymously)

No.............$\square_0$ ➔ [If no, go to Question **12**]

Yes.............$\square_1$

When surveys are administered by face-to-face interviewers, respondents can be asked to respond to a sensitive question on a computer or on a pen-and-paper portion of the interview. The latter can be placed in an envelope and marked with an identification number.

The placement of sensitive questions near the end of the survey will give the respondent time to gain trust in the survey instrument before being confronted with sensitive issues. Question wording may also affect whether and how a respondent answers. 'Yes/no' responses provide an easy opportunity for respondents to respond 'no' to, say, marijuana use. Less restrictive response categories, such as a scale, or an open-ended question, may be interpreted as less judgemental and hence more inviting of an honest response.

A word about international comparative research

Wordsmithing in one language is difficult enough. Even in comparative projects in a single language such as English, concepts and terminology across different jurisdictions may be very different. For example, attempting to design a question measuring highest level of education attained in Canada, the United States, the United Kingdom, Australia, and New Zealand would be challenged by differing conceptions of educational attainment (e.g., leaving school at age 16 is considered valid in the UK; in Canada and the USA, without having completed Grade 12, one is considered a 'drop-out').

TEXT BOX 5.3

International comparative research

It is particularly challenging to construct survey items to be meaningful across cultures and language groups. Plan on budgeting for extra resources for question construction, translation, and piloting.

International comparative research involving more than one language group, for example the English-speaking world and the German-speaking world, adds another level of challenge in writing comparable questions. The resources required for such research may be considerable and must be built in to research budgets to ensure that comparative survey research is indeed comparative. Extensive piloting of survey items is essential.

Layout, formatting, and design

After the questions have been designed, issues of layout, formatting, and design of the survey must be addressed. In self-administered surveys, the survey instrument is designed to guide the respondent in answering the questions. In interviewer-administered surveys, the instrument is designed to assist the interviewer through the interview process. First, I will address issues that are relevant regardless of mode of administration. Second, I will comment on format-specific issues.

Question order

Questions should be grouped according to theme. At the beginning of this chapter I began by indicating that survey questions should be written in relation to the research questions of the study. The research questions may provide a logical order for the sequencing of questions into sections. Also, an introduction to each section can be provided to help guide the respondent.

Within sections of a survey, some questions may be free-standing, and others may form a series (see Example 5.17). Converse and Presser (1986: 41) suggest a funnel approach to question order, with general questions preceding specific questions.

Often, it is intentional that answers to questions are contingent upon answers to earlier questions; however, it is possible that answers to one or more questions may introduce unintended bias in answers to subsequent questions. Such bias can be reduced or eliminated by avoiding loaded words in question stems and response categories.

Skip instructions

All questions contained in a survey may not be relevant to all respondents. When it is necessary to direct respondents to a question that does not follow from the previous one, it is critical to provide clear 'skip instructions'. Failure to include clear skip instructions may result in failure by respondents to complete portions of the questionnaire or failure by interviewers to be directed to the relevant parts of the questionnaire. Web surveys have the advantage of being able to program skip questions so that the respondent is automatically directed to the next relevant question.

Piloting

The need for piloting individual survey items and the entire survey instrument cannot be stressed enough. Survey questions can be piloted first with colleagues, friends, and family who can assume the roles of specific and general audiences. Once the questionnaire is in reasonable shape, it can be piloted with individuals, focus groups, or both. The piloting process should be a test of each of the following components of the survey: salience of the questions; the clarity of individual words and individual questions; the nature of the stems and response categories; the scales employed; skip instructions; redundant or absent questions. For pen-and-paper and web surveys, the attractiveness of the layout should also be assessed by those piloting the instrument.

Proofreading for technical accuracy

The penultimate facet of survey design is to proofread the instrument to eliminate any technical mistakes. Mistakes such as typographical errors or awkward grammar or syntax may raise issues of credibility with the respondent. The survey instrument needs to be technically perfect. To accomplish this, one or more professional proofreaders may be required. Finally, the survey questions should be entered into the appropriate analytical software package as a last check for any design flaws (see Chapter 9).

Mode-specific issues

In Chapter 2, the different survey modes were specified in considerable detail. There are, however, a few additional considerations regarding item and questionnaire design that will vary depending on the mode employed.

Self-administered mail surveys

Self-administered surveys, whether in the form of pen-and-paper or web surveys, rely on the ability of the respondent to read, interpret, and respond to survey items. The survey instrument should be designed in a visually appealing way.

Pen-and-paper surveys

Pen-and-paper surveys should include considerable white space. That is, questions should not be crammed into the smallest space possible. The use of colour can greatly enhance the appearance of a survey and help to guide respondents through it.

Web surveys

With the aid of software supplied by web survey providers, it is easy to create an attractive survey instrument. However, web surveys must be tested on several browsers to ensure that the layout appears as intended. Also, the extent to which the survey demands computer resources such as speed and memory must be accounted for in relation to the intended audience.

The issue of forcing respondents to answer all questions in a web survey must be considered carefully. Although it is desirable from the researcher's perspective that all relevant questions are answered, forcing respondents to respond to all questions – through, for example, not allowing them to proceed to the next question without answering the current one – may result in either inaccurate responses or in frustration and even abandonment of the task altogether.

Interviewer-administered surveys

With interviewer-administered surveys, the survey instrument must be designed in a way that allows the interviewer to read the text and record responses easily while engaging the respondent in the interview conversation. The text must be large enough to read, and the skip instructions must be clear to the interviewer. Also, words that are difficult to pronounce should be substituted for simpler words.

When the number of interviews conducted is small, it may be desirable to digitally record the interview. Advances in voice recognition software such as Dragon have greatly reduced the time and cost of transcribing interviews.

Telephone surveys

Telephone surveys present the most challenges in terms of questionnaire delivery. In particular, scales that can be used easily in other modes must be modified for a telephone survey. Rather than employing response categories with five, seven, or even ten categories, it is recommended that in telephone surveys, scales should contain only three or four categories. Otherwise, respondents will lose track and may remember, and hence respond, to the first or last category (Fowler, 1995: 53).

Face-to-face surveys

Because the interviewer is physically present, s/he may use aids in the form of scales, charts, or any other visual that might help the respondent to understand the questions. The interviewer must be well versed with the content of the survey in order to engage the interviewee in a conversation. The interviewer must also be skilled in reading body language and other visual cues such as pauses or hesitation in answering questions, and employ techniques such as silence, repeating the question, clarifying terms that are not understood or misunderstood, and using the technique of probing to elicit more complete responses.

Summary

In this chapter, through the use of numerous examples, the spectrum of survey question formats was portrayed. Guiding principles for question construction were specified and examples of good and poor questions were presented. Common pitfalls to be avoided in question design were emphasized. The chapter concluded by highlighting format-specific issues.

Exercises

1 Develop the survey instrument to be used in your survey project. Use the information provided in this chapter to select question formats that are appropriate for the questions at hand.

2 Prepare two versions of your survey from the following: mail-out survey, telephone survey, face-to-face survey, online survey using a mixed methods approach.

3 Conduct a pilot of your survey instruments.

Further reading

Converse, J. M., and Presser, S. (1986). *Survey Questions: Handcrafting the Standardized Questionnaire.* Thousand Oaks, CA: Sage.

Lazarsfeld, P. (1944). The controversy over detailed interviews: An offer for negotiation. *Public Opinion Quarterly,* 8(1), 38–60.

Payne, S. (1951). *The Art of Asking Questions.* Princeton, NJ: Princeton University Press.

SIX

Sampling theory and practice

By the time you are ready to construct a sample, you will have already made a series of decisions. Some decisions will either affect the eventual sample or have been affected by your initial choice of a sample. Sampling decisions – even if preliminary – usually emerge early in the inception of a study and may indeed drive the design. Sampling decisions involve trade-offs among three things: what you as the researcher want to do, what you are able to do (in terms of time and resources) and what you are allowed to do. These decisions are shaped by the limits you impose on the survey research project, known as the *delimitations* of a study, and on the *limitations* imposed by others (e.g., access to a given sample). In almost all instances, regardless of the type of sampling strategy chosen, samples are volunteer samples. That is, according to today's ethics protocols, individuals cannot be coerced, or even seduced by incentives so enticing that they feel compelled to participate. In rare instances, for example censuses of the population, participation is mandatory and can be enforced by threats of fines or imprisonment. However, even such coercion in these rare instances is highly controversial.

Sampling strategies can make or break a study.

TEXT BOX 6.1

Ethics Alert!

All samples are volunteer samples – individuals must agree to participate in the study. National censuses are the only exceptions.

This chapter begins with an overview of populations and samples followed by a description of sampling strategies and sources of error. I provide a detailed account of the different approaches to non-probabilistic sampling and probabilistic sampling strategies. I demonstrate how different strategies can be combined to strengthen the explanatory power of a study. Errors due to sampling frame issues, sampling, non-response, and other sources of error, sample size determination and related issues of power are highlighted. Ethical concerns around certain types of sampling strategies (e.g., snowball sampling) are highlighted.

Initially, all survey research begins from the purposive stance of the researcher. That is, judgements about what is and what is not important to study are used to conceptualize the initial stages of the survey research design and most often these same judgements shape every step of the decision process. There is a misconception in the literature that research, including sampling strategies, can and should be disembodied from the minds and hands of the researchers. It is not unusual to see statements such as 'sampling should be done in such a way that the researcher has no influence on the selection of respondents; otherwise the researcher can influence the results' (Saris and Gallhofer, 2007: 10). Every decision by the researcher influences the results – for example, the decision to include only men, only women, or both will determine the extent of comparability of men and women.

All sampling decisions are by nature multi-stage and begin by the examination of theory, previous research, available historical and archival data, and detailed literature reviews. In doing so, the researcher gains 'an in-depth working knowledge of that population and must enumerate the units that make it up' (Denzin, 1989: 72) to 'develop sharper and more insightful *questions* about the topic' (Yin, 1989: 20). Sampling procedures provide guidelines or a set of rules for making sound decisions based on this melange of information. The rules are used to construct a study to produce findings that can be extended – either by *generalizing* the findings to a larger population, or by *transferring* the findings to other settings and samples.

There are two approaches to sampling. Non-probabilistic sampling is based on judgements made by the researcher, and probabilistic sampling employs random selection to generate a list of study participants. All studies, whether they are large-scale studies employing probabilistic sampling designs or small-scale studies employing judgement samples, must identify the following: the **population**, the **target population**, the **sampling frame**, the **survey sample**, and the **respondents**. Related to each of these steps are considerations of the sources of error that must be identified and disclosed in any rigorous research project. Although these steps are always part of a study involving probabilistic sampling, often they are not made explicit, ignored, or even dismissed by researchers conducting smaller-scale studies that employ non-probabilistic sampling designs. It is essential for all survey research projects to engage in this level of disclosure. In doing so, the extent to which the findings can be generalized or transferred can be determined. Too often, researchers claim that they do not intend their findings to be generalizable, but in fact report the findings as if they are indeed generalizable.

Below, the target population, the sampling frame, the survey sample, and the study respondents are described.

Populations and samples

Target population

The population is the highest level of abstraction in a study. However, even the most perfectly constructed sample has its limits in terms of generalizability or transferability. Instead, we aim to identify a target population – one to which the study can be realistically generalizable or transferable. Considerable effort must be spent to define a given target population by understanding, in detail, its nature and characteristics. Here, the approach that Charles Booth followed in the early 1900s is instructive. In order to grasp an understanding of the population of London, he studied, among other sources, Poor Law statistics, information collected on families by school visitors, and police reports of registered lodging houses, and carried out 'focus groups' to understand the issues facing the population. Today, a vast array of information is available, including census data, Chamber of Commerce reports, and demographic descriptions about given communities of interest. Analyses of existing information helps the researcher to provide a workable and operational definition (Denzin, 1989: 72) of the population. At this point, the researcher decides whether the scope of the project warrants using the entire population or *census,* or whether some type of sampling strategy is preferable. Although samples are often more affordable and can be surveyed more quickly and easily, entire populations may be more appealing and may result in less bias when collecting data for certain types of studies (Kish, 1967).

To further define the population, first the individual units of analysis must be specified. The second level to be identified is the *grouping unit,* which could be a household, an organization, or a school. Third, the *geographic boundaries* and possible *strata* or subclasses of individuals must be specified. The former are physical boundaries and the latter are often demographic boundaries such as gender, income groups, and ethnic or racial categories. And fourth, the *time period* must be specified. In other words, the population is defined by *who* is the focus of the study together with delimiting and limiting components at every level of the study.

Example 6.1 demonstrates how a population is transformed from a vague definition to a workable, operational entity. In carrying out these steps, individuals who are *eligible* to participate in the study will be defined in relation to those who are deemed *ineligible.* In addition, comparative components can be added, for example, comparing two or more organizations or countries.

Example 6.1 Defining the sample

	Elements	Grouping Unit	Geographic Boundary	Strata	Time
	Who	What	Where	Who (specifics)	When
Less specific	librarians	public libraries	large cities	all	autumn
More specific	librarians	main public libraries	cities with populations > 500,000	gender age groups educational attainment	October– November

Important ethical considerations also guide sampling decisions. All studies require some form of consent from the responding individual. However, some individuals, such as minors and those who are incapable of providing informed consent (e.g., the physically or mentally challenged), either will not be able to be included in the study, will require consent from somebody else (e.g., parent or guardian), or will be asked to provide assent (agreement to participate) together with consent from somebody else.

TEXT BOX 6.2

Ethics Alert!

'Consent' means that permission to participate in a research project has been granted by a participant who is competent to do so. Parents must provide consent for children who are under age. Children must also agree to participate by providing 'assent'.

Sampling frame

Once the individual units of analysis, grouping units, geographic units, strata, and time parameters have been delineated, the sampling frame can be devised. By defining the target population, the sampling frame may have already been defined. However, a few more stages of refinement may be required which are again driven by the delimitations and limitations of the study. For example, in a study of elementary schools in a given province or state, or perhaps even an entire country, it may be feasible to include all schools within all school districts. However, the feasibility of conducting the study – in terms of time and money and resources available at schools and districts – may require the sample to be narrowed further. At this point, complete lists of the individuals and related contact information (mailing addresses, email addresses) is not necessarily required. Instead, lists of grouping units may be sufficient. However, once the grouping units have been designed, then complete listings of all individuals from whom to draw the sample must be constructed.

Sometimes, lists of individuals are readily available. For example, it may be relatively easy to gain access to lists of employees in a given corporation or lists of members of professional associations. However, obtaining lists from which samples can be generated can become extremely complex. For example, the website of the Association of Universities and Colleges in Canada (http://www.aucc.ca/) contains an extensive searchable database of universities and courses. If one wished to construct a sample of doctoral students in Canada, such a database would provide a first step. However, once Canadian universities with doctoral programmes are identified, negotiation for lists of students would have to be carried out with individual universities. Clearly, issues of privacy and confidentiality will arise and each university has its own set of ethics regulations about releasing such information (for an extended discussion of ethics boards and survey research on university students, see Grayson and Myles, 2004). A positive scenario might be that a university may agree to carry out a survey on behalf of the researcher. However, this involves additional resources on the part of a university to construct samples and administer the survey. Conducting such a research project on a large scale – for example a large representative sample of universities in Canada – may, simply for reasons of cost and practicality, need to be scaled down to two or three institutions or even to specific doctoral programmes (e.g., in departments of economics) within these universities.

Lists themselves can be fraught with problems. As Kish (1967: 53) explains, 'the frame is perfect if every element [individual] appears on the list separately, once, only once, and nothing else appears on the list. In other words: every element must appear in a listing, and only in one listing; also, every list must contain an element, and only one element'. Lists are often incomplete or flawed in other ways, and these flaws should be determined and remedied if possible. Problems with lists and approaches to improve the quality of lists are taken up at the end of this chapter.

Not all sampling strategies involve the generation of lists of individuals. As we shall see shortly, it may not be necessary to have comprehensive lists of individuals for convenience samples. Strategies such as snowball sampling are employed precisely because it may be impossible to obtain lists of certain populations.

Survey sample

The term 'survey sample' is used here in the generic rather than in a probabilistic sense to refer to the subset of individuals that are generated from a list. In the example above, a sample may be drawn from a list of doctoral students in departments of economics at three major universities.

Respondents

Finally, respondents are those individuals from the survey sample who respond to the survey. Not all respondents who are recruited to participate in a study are able or willing to participate. The various forms of non-response are additional sources of error contributing to the extent to which the findings generated from the respondents can shed light on the target population of interest.

Sampling approaches

All sampling approaches begin from a non-probabilistic perspective. Judgements and decisions such as in which country to locate the study, what topic, what institution, organization or other grouping unit, and the demographic make-up of the study's participants, and whether the study involves census or a sample, all require judgement calls that are based on considerations such as the researcher's interests, expertise, the time available to complete the study, funding based on research money, requirements of a sponsor, to name a few. In addition, the balance between survey errors and the cost of conducting a study may warrant the choice of non-probability over probability sampling. Most textbooks discourage or dismiss the use of non-probability sampling and often do not present alternative sampling strategies. However, it may not be feasible or desirable to employ a probability sampling strategy. As Kish (1967: 29) points out, 'probability sampling for randomization is not a dogma but a strategy' and 'no clear rule exists for deciding exactly when probability sampling is necessary, and what price should be paid for it'.

The best sampling strategy for a given survey project is the one that is best suited to the study. As indicated above, there are many criteria that come into play when defining 'best'. For small-scale research projects, probability sampling is either not necessary, not feasible, and/or not desirable. Also, the tenets of ethics may dictate what can or cannot be done in terms of sampling. I begin this section with a discussion of non-probability sampling.

Non-probabilistic sampling strategies

Non-probability sampling does not employ a random selection process. Rather, these strategies require the judgement of the researcher to select the sample. Non-probability samples are often condemned as being 'subjective' and not 'scientific'. However, by employing sound sampling practices and documenting in detail the sampling procedures employed, non-probabilistic sampling procedures will produce findings that can be transferable to other studies.

There is, however, a difference between *haphazard* and *purposive* sampling strategies. Haphazard samples are constructed without attempting to match the sample to the research questions at hand. Kish (1967: 18) asserts that researchers 'assume, vaguely and implicitly, that "typical items" were chosen. They hope that the important characteristics are distributed either uniformly or randomly in the population'. Purposive sampling involves the intentional, careful selection and matching of the sample to the study. Even probabilistic sampling can be conducted in a thoughtless haphazard way. For example, using a stratified random sample drawn from a subject pool comprised of psychology undergraduate students makes sense only if the purpose of the research is relevant and related to the characteristics of undergraduate students at that given university. The major limitation of non-probability sampling is that it is not possible to estimate sampling error, and hence the biases in a study due to sampling cannot be determined statistically. However, as I discuss later in this chapter, calculating sampling error in studies employing probabilistic sampling designs is not unproblematic and only identifies one of several types of potential errors in a survey research project.

Below, I describe the various types of non-probability samples. Although I treat each type of sample discretely, they are not necessarily so, and it is also possible to combine non-probability and probability sampling.

Convenience or availability samples

Convenience or availability samples simply draw on what is convenient or available. A typical example is a university classroom of students. This sample is easily accessible and able to participate in a survey research project. Subject pools of university students are also convenience samples.

At some level, most studies are convenience samples. As Weisberg (2005: 234) points out,

> at the extreme, surveys of one's own country can be considered to be instances of convenience samples. Social scientists are generally trying to develop generalizations that are not country specific, but they usually take surveys only in their own country because of costs as well as limited funding possibilities. Thus many surveys that appear to be probability samples are in this sense actually availability samples.

Convenience in terms of geographic proximity, familiarity, issues of language, and knowledge of cultural norms and mores play into the design of any study.

Convenience sampling is used initially to identify the grouping unit or unit of analysis of the study. Once one or more grouping units are identified, then either all individuals within the group (census) or a non-random or random sample of individuals is recruited to participate.

A convenience sample is appropriate and the findings will be meaningful if the sample is appropriate for the question at hand. For example, conducting an in-class pen-and-paper survey of first-year undergraduate students about the quality of food services at their university would meet the criteria of appropriateness. Surveying the same sample about their voting preferences in an upcoming referendum on tax reform would not produce very meaningful or unbiased results as the sample is poorly suited to the question.

Volunteer samples

Almost all studies are volunteer samples in that it is unethical to force or overly coerce individuals to participate in a research project. However, some studies are constructed to recruit volunteers who may or may not be representative of the larger population of interest. Capturing people as they exit a bar, a polling station, or a shop to participate in an on-the-spot survey are all examples of volunteer sampling, as are phone-in surveys and voluntary internet newspaper surveys. Technology such as voluntary internet polling may generate large samples, but the results of such studies will not be very meaningful in terms of using the findings to explain a given topic. One only needs to read the voluntary comments about any given newspaper article or to listen to a 'phone-in' radio programme to see that particular types of people, who are probably not representative of the population at large, are more likely to respond. Such individuals are 'self-selected'. As Bradburn and Sudman (1988: 7) indicate, the validity of surveys based on self-selection is not at all legitimate in that such samples are often disguised as ones that have been carefully constructed using sound survey sampling principles. As such, they would fall under the category of haphazard sampling.

However, volunteer samples within a convenience context – say, recruiting volunteers from a community centre – are bounded by 'place' and hence can be contextualized to give the findings more meaning.

Intercept polls

Intercept polls are similar to volunteer samples in that potential survey participants are approached in a particular location. However, if they involve surveying every *i*th person, for example, as they leave a polling station during an election, and if probabilistic sampling strategies can be employed to choose the sampling locations, this sampling strategy is considered to be a more systematic sampling approach. However, this strategy is subject to interviewer bias in that the *i*th person may be deemed by the survey interviewer to be undesirable or unapproachable.

In-person delivery samples

This 'foot-in-the door' (Dillman, 2000: 246) approach is a combination of a convenience and an intercept sample. A convenient location, (e.g., a museum or a cultural event such as the Oktoberfest in Bavaria) is chosen. Interviewers wait until potential study participants exit a venue. Then, in the spirit of an intercept sample, every *i*th person is approached and asked to participate in a survey. The interviewer is able to explain the study and to ask a member of a party of more than one person to serve as the designated survey participant. At this point, either the survey is given to the person who agreed to complete it, or s/he can be asked for a mailing address to which the survey can be sent. Dillman (2000) provides detailed examples of this approach.

Volunteer opt-in panels (access panels)

A voluntary opt-in panel or access panel is a sampling strategy to recruit individuals to participate in online surveys. The sample is recruited through banners, pop-up advertisements, or other forms of online recruiting and may involve a *single opt-in* or a *double opt-in* approach. In single opt-in recruiting, potential panel participants who have responded to recruitment methods such as banners are redirected to a specific panel recruitment portal and are asked to supply demographic information, including an email address. In double opt-in recruiting, after having responded to a banner or some other recruitment strategy, potential participants are sent a confirmation email with a link that, once clicked, enrols them in the panel. The individual then becomes part of an active panel and will be called upon from time to time to participate in a survey. Membership in the panel may be time-limited and members who do not participate regularly may be purged from the database (Callegaro and DiSogra, 2008; Postoaca, 2006; Sue and Ritter, 2007). A description of the use of opt-in panels in polling research can be found on the Ipsos Reid website (http://www.ipsos-na.com/products-tools/public-affairs/public-opinion-research-using-online-panels/).

Cases

All studies involve one or more cases of *something* – countries, organizations, or hospitals within a health board system. The term 'case' can be employed to describe the grouping unit or unit of analysis described earlier in this chapter. For example, Blossfield and Timm (2003) is an edited volume of country cases for which large-scale survey data exist. Or it can have a very specific meaning as in 'case study', which is a research strategy in and of itself which may employ survey research as one data collection tool. Yin (1989: 23) describes the case study method as *'an empirical study that:* investigates a contemporary phenomenon within its real-life context; when the boundaries between phenomenon and context are not clearly evident; and in which multiple sources of evidence are used'. The term 'case' can mean many things, including events, entities, programmes, or organizational change (Yin, 1989). Defining the case requires multiple purposive judgement calls on the part of the researcher. *Typical, critical, extreme* case and *revelatory* study designs are examples.

Typical cases

A typical case study design is the weakest in terms of meeting the definition specified by Yin. In attempting to choose a typical case, the researcher is striving to find a case that is 'representative', 'normal', or 'usual'. However, as Kish (1967: 29) points out, the purposive choice of a typical case may be preferable over a random approach:

> if a research project must be confined to a single city in the US, I would rather use my judgment to choose a 'typical' city than select one at random. Even for a sample of 10 cities, I would rather trust my knowledge of US cities than a random selection.

Researchers must use their judgement and specify criteria on which to determine that a case is indeed 'typical'. The term 'typical' is problematic in that what might be typical when seen through a given conceptual lens or in one particular situation may not be typical in other respects. Criticisms by Igo (2007) of the *Middletown* research project of Robert and Helen Lynd highlight the difficulties surrounding the notion of 'typical'.

Critical cases

A critical case study design sets out to test a well-formulated theory (Yin, 1989). In order to do so, the chosen case must meet all of the conditions to 'test ... confirm, challenge or extend the theory' (p. 47). For example, in an examination of educational theories of early or late selection of students into various academic tracks, countries such as Austria and Germany could be chosen as cases of early selection, and Canada and the USA as examples of late selection. Surveys such as those administered in conjunction with the OECD Programme for International

Student Assessment collect demographic data on students. This mixed method design (i.e., assessments and surveys) can be used to test theory.

Extreme or deviant cases

An extreme or deviant case design focuses on a rare or extremely unusual instance of the phenomenon of interest. A case study of earthquake survivors with one or more survey components serves as an example.

Similar/dissimilar cases

In a similar/dissimilar design, two or more cases are chosen for their maximal similarity or maximal dissimilarity to each other. Such a design can seek *maximum variation* by examining important differences and commonalities can focus on the extent to which cases serve to confirm or disconfirm certain phenomena (Miles and Huberman, 1994: 28) or can highlight 'best' and 'worst' policy strategies or practices (Henry, 1990: 20). An example of this approach would be to employ Esping-Andersen's (1990, 1999, 2009) welfare regime typology to examine how clusters of countries differ in terms of social welfare policies.

Once one or more cases are identified, many survey research sampling strategies may be employed to gather information. For example, in a case study of a large corporation, a stratified random sample of employers may be generated in order to conduct a pen-and-paper survey, and a snowball sampling strategy (see below) may be used to identify and carry out face-to-face interviews with the power brokers in the company. A case study design can be strengthened by using a comparative approach.

Snowball samples

A snowball research design may be employed when participants are either difficult to locate (e.g., HIV-positive pregnant intravenous drug users living in an inner city) or are part of specialized group of individuals (e.g., members of elite political networks).

TEXT BOX 6.3

Ethics Alert!

When employing a snowball sample, be sure to meet the requirements of the appropriate behavioural review boards.

Gaining access to such samples often requires some level of insider knowledge. In order to gain access to members of certain populations, an initial site would need to be identified and some sort of initial recruitment strategy employed. For example, recruitment posters could be displayed at safe injection sites. Also, for example, health care or law enforcement staff could be asked to disseminate information about the study. Once one or more respondents who meet the criteria of the study are located, they become recruiters for more respondents by helping to identify others who meet the criteria of the study and who are 'information rich' (Miles and Huberman, 1994: 28). However, ethics protocols are key in such studies. It is no longer feasible to ask respondents to provide names and contact information of potential participants as this violates the principles of privacy. Instead, the researcher would provide information to the participant-recruiter who would then pass it on to other potential participants. The latter would contact the researcher directly.

Quota samples

Quota sampling is a technique employed to gather data from individuals in the same proportion as they are represented in the population. Available census and other sources of information are used to define the population of interest according to certain criteria. Such criteria often include gender, age, and racial/ethnic group. Quotas of the strata of interest are then specified and the researcher or team of researchers will strive to fill the quotas.

Quota sampling does not employ probability sampling. Rather than selecting individuals for inclusion in the study based on random sampling, individuals are approached – either face-to-face, by telephone, or through the internet – and are screened in terms of the criteria of the study. If the individual meets the criteria, s/he is included and data gathering proceeds in this way until the quotas are filled.

The major weakness of quota sampling is that it allows the researcher to determine whom to include in the study. It is possible, or even likely, that in a face-to-face situation researchers will approach potential participants whom they perceive to be more willing to participate and who do not pose a threat, either verbally or physically, to the researcher. A study employing quota samples may be efficient in that the quotas are filled in a reasonable length of time. However, because of the judgement calls of the researcher, the sample may be biased because certain individuals may not have been approached to participate in the study. The sample may be additionally biased due to the location of the study. For example, university libraries may be full of young adults; however, clearly those individuals frequenting university libraries are not representative of the general population of young adults.

Criticisms of this approach are often based on assumption that interviewers are employees who may take shortcuts to fill their quotas. In small-scale research where data are collected by the researcher or a small team of researchers, it is in the interest of the research team to ensure that the desired representativeness is captured. In an appropriate setting, quota sampling may be as effective as a probability sample. Despite voicing numerous concerns about quota sampling, Kish (1967: 565) concedes that, for example, 'a quota sample is more likely to represent the attitude of the nation's young people, than a probability sample of college students'.

Another approach is to generate the sample, first, using probability sampling and then using quota sampling to select the sample. The probability of an individual being included in the sample is 'the product of his [sic] initial selection probability times his probability of being available for interviewing' (Sudman, 1976: 193). However, this approach requires that the probability of being available to participate in the study is known.

Summary

Non-probability sampling is common in survey research. With non-probability sampling strategies, the researcher uses her/his judgement to select the sample. There are a myriad of non-sampling approaches from which to choose. The sampling strategy should be chosen to select research participants who are best able to accurately and meaningfully provide responses to your survey instrument. Researchers employing non-probability sampling strategies should document carefully the sample selection process. Issues of subjectivity that may affect sample selection and efforts to safeguard against it, if appropriate, should be revealed. The extent to which the findings can be generalized or transferred to other settings and samples should also be addressed.

Probabilistic sampling

The key feature of probability samples is that each unit in the population has a known, non-zero probability of being included in the sample. To generate a probability sample, some form of random selection is used. Today, such samples are usually generated with the aid of a computer program. However, numbers corresponding to the names and contact information of individuals could be drawn from a hat as in a lottery. Also central to probabilistic sampling is the tenet that each selection is independent of the others; that is, by selecting one individual for inclusion, the likelihood of selecting another individual is not affected.

It is important to point out that before one can engage in a probability sampling strategy, a series of non-probabilistic decisions must be made. Decisions about the purpose of the study, and often the site or sites (e.g., country, institutions) are determined non-probabilistically. In other words, every study requires a series of sampling decisions, many of which are purposive. Often along the way, constraints in getting the sample one wants are encountered. Ethical issues, political processes, or both can prevent the 'ideal' study from being constructed.

Census

A census is a sample of the entire population, or a sample which has 100% probability of being selected. However, a census is still considered a sample rather than a population for two reasons. First, a census exists only at a particular moment in time and space. Even in censuses of an entire country, fluctuations due to births, deaths, and immigration mean the population will vary from one day to the next. Second, a census is subject to errors such as inability or refusal to participate or inaccuracies in lists of the population (Kish, 1967: 18).

Simple random samples

Simple random sampling is the most basic of probabilistic sampling designs. To produce a simple random sample, first the population must be defined, the proportion of the population is determined, and then that proportion of the elements (individuals) are chosen randomly from the population.The probability of selection is as follows:

n represents the number of units in the sample

N represents the number of units in the study population

p is the probability of selection

f is the sampling fraction.

In a simple random sample, each subset of n units is equally to be selected from the N units of the population. The probability of selection for each member of the study population is

$$p = f = n/N$$

For example, in a study, 3020 individuals were randomly selected from the 22,556 members for whom names and addresses were available. The probability of selection is 3020/22,556 or 0.13

Despite its simple mathematical appeal, simple random sampling is rarely used in real-world research. The limitations of such a sampling strategy are threefold: (1) in order to generate a simple random sample, the entire list of the population of interest must be accessible to the researcher, which is often not the case; (2) such a design is expensive, especially when a study involves large geographic regions and face-to-face interviews (Weisberg, 2005: 238); and (3) small random samples may not be representative of the population in that certain groups (e.g., small racial or ethnic populations) may be under-represented or not represented.

Systematic random samples

Systematic random sampling, also known as 'pseudo-random selection' (Kish, 1967: 113) is an efficient approach to extracting names from lists. The first element is selected randomly, followed by the selection of every *i*th element on the list. With *n* and *N* defined as for simple random sampling, the *sampling interval, i,* is

$$i = N/n$$

For example, if one wants a sample of 1250 from a population list of 5000 individuals, after initial selection by a random start, every fourth individual would be selected.

Systematic sampling does not escape any of the limitations identified under simple random sampling, and may indeed introduce different types of error into the study. The population list must be scrutinized for evidence of *monotonic trends* and *periodic fluctuations* (Kish, 1967: 120). A *monotonic trend* occurs when the population list is ordered cyclically, and 'the cycle coincides with the sample selection' (Henry, 1990). For example, lists could be ordered by birth date or alphabetically which then correspond with the *i*th element of selection. In a school district in which elementary classrooms are comprised of 30 students who are listed from youngest to oldest by birth date, an interval of 25 would pick students who were more likely to be older and therefore not representative of the intended sample. *Periodic fluctuations* occur, for example, during the ebbs and flows of business cycles. These problems are deemed to be rare and can be resolved by either randomizing the population list or changing the random start several times during the process (Kish, 1967).

Stratified random samples

A stratified random sample introduces more precision into the sampling design. Instead of selecting a sample from the entire population, first the sample is divided into subgroups or strata. The strata must be identified in advance based on information that is available for all units. The criteria for defining the strata should be meaningful to the study. Each unit is assigned to one and only one stratum. Strata can be simple – such as dividing the sample into two groups of women and men – or more complex, for example, six strata by two gender categories and three educational categories. Table 6.1 provides an example. Here, females represent 1592/3020 = 53% and males 1428/3020 = 47% of the total sample.

Once individuals are assigned to each stratum – for example, 204 females with low levels of education – independent random samples are selected from each stratum either by employing a simple random sampling or systematic sampling procedure.

When assigning units to strata, either a *proportionate* or *disproportionate stratification* process can be employed. With *proportionate stratification*, or equal probability of selection, the number of cases sampled from each stratum is proportional to the relative size of the stratum. In Table 6.1, a 25% sample is drawn from each stratum, which corresponds with the relative size of each stratum. A *disproportionate stratification* or unequal probability of selection process can be used when some strata are likely to be under-represented due to their small size or are less likely to participate in the study. Usually, oversampling is employed. In the example in Table 6.1, a 50% sample is selected from two groups (e.g., females with low levels of education and males with high levels of education) who may be less likely to participate in the study. By oversampling, the goal is to achieve a response rate similar to those from other strata.

Table 6.1 Random, proportionate, and disproportionate sampling strategies

	N	Random sample	25% Proportionate sample	Disproportionate sample to overselect females with low education and males with high education
Females, low education	204	26 (13%)	51 (25%)	102 (50%)
Females, medium education	896	151 (17%)	224 (25%)	224 (25%)
Females, high education	492	120 (24%)	123 (25%)	123 (25%)
Males, low education	636	187 (30%)	159 (25%)	159 (25%)
Males, medium education	444	132 (30%)	111 (25%)	111 (25%)
Males, high education	348	139 (40%)	87 (25%)	174 (50%)

SURVEYS-R-US

87% OF THE 56% WHO COMPLETED MORE
THAN 23% OF THE SURVEY THOUGHT IT

Cartoon 6.1

Although stratified samples allow for more precision in the sampling design by reducing the sampling error, Weisberg (2005: 240) warns that with disproportionate sampling 'the variance within strata will be different for different variables, which means that the optimal allocation for disproportionate sampling can vary between variables'. Hence, disproportionate stratification should be used with caution as it may result in an increase, rather than a decrease, in sampling error 'if poor guesses are made about the proportions to use, as would happen if more cases were selected from strata with less variance on the variables of interest' (p. 240).

Cluster samples

Cluster sampling is an efficient and cost-effective way of sampling. This sampling strategy is most useful when clusters are naturally-occurring groupings such as schools, hospitals, or other types of organization. The cluster, and not the individual member of the unit of analysis, becomes the unit of analysis, and the clusters selected are considered representative of the population. As with other forms of sampling, lists of 'clusters' must be available. For example, in a study of senior secondary students in a given school district, a list of all schools within the district containing senior secondary classrooms must be available. The clusters to be included in the study are randomly selected, and each member of the cluster is included in the sample. A systematic sampling strategy can be employed, but in doing so the list must be scrutinized for any cyclical trends (e.g., class lists ordered by grade point average). To add more precision, lists can be stratified, for example into small, medium, and large high schools, or by the socioeconomic composition of the area surrounding each school, followed by a random sampling process from each stratum. Proportionate or disproportionate sampling strategies can be employed.

Multi-stage cluster samples

Multi-stage cluster samples are constructed by employing two or more layers of cluster sampling in the design. In the first step, clusters are generated as described above. In this type of design, the first level of clusters are called *primary sampling units.* To extend the senior secondary classrooms example, we could begin at the level of school districts and include all school districts in one province or state of a country. The primary sampling units in the study would be the school districts that are randomly selected from the population of districts. For example, a given province or state is comprised of 80 districts and the researchers wish to include ten districts in their study. Once the ten districts are selected, a *secondary sampling unit* of schools is drawn randomly from each district. At this point, either all senior secondary classrooms could be included in the study, or a random sample of classrooms could be drawn. At any stage in the design, stratified sampling and disproportionate sampling can be introduced. For example, to increase precision, the school districts in the study could be stratified by population density, and then a sample could be drawn from each stratum.

Cluster sampling has several advantages over other forms of sampling. First, in the initial stages, entire lists of individuals are not required. Second, the study will be concentrated in particular geographic regions, which may lower the overall costs of data collection. In the senior secondary classrooms example, the study is confined to a few schools rather than a few students in all schools as would be the case in a stratified sampling design. In the case of pen-and-paper questionnaires, mail-out costs can be reduced by sending a package of survey materials to the school or by sending one person to administer the questionnaires to classrooms of students. In the case of face-to-face interviews, travelling costs of interviewers are reduced because only a few schools are involved. Third, because the clusters are selected randomly, this design is deemed to meet the criteria of a probability sample.

However, there is one major disadvantage to this design. That is, clusters tend to be homogeneous. For example, students in a given school may be more homogeneous in terms of socioeconomic background than students from the schools in a wider area. Hence, the clusters drawn may not be representative of the population. Also, the researchers may be unaware of certain peculiarities of a cluster that make it unique rather than typical of the population. As a result, element variance is greater in cluster samples than in studies relying on a sample of elements. At the end of this chapter I point out that it may be more reasonable to employ the non-probabilistic sampling strategy of 'typical' cases to reduce the chance of choosing atypical clusters. This problem can be solved by a detailed examination of the population of clusters *a priori*.

Summary

When the goal is to employ a smaller sample to generalize to a target population, a probabilistic sampling strategy is often the best means to do so. Various approaches, all based on the tenet of random sampling, are available to the researcher. Decisions regarding the choice of approach will be determined by the research questions, availability of accurate and complete lists of individuals (see the next section), and often a substantial research budget.

Errors and corrections

Several types of errors may occur during the sampling process. These errors can be categorized as *non-sampling* errors, *sampling* errors, *measurement* errors, and *non-response* errors. Kish (1967) offers a general rule of thumb when dealing with error: (1) If the problem is small and not considered to bias the study in any meaningful way, it can be ignored. (2) If the sampling frame is highly flawed, it may be necessary to 'redefine the problem to fit the frame' (p. xx). This solution is viable only if it makes sense in terms of the purpose of the study or if the purpose of the study can be redefined to align with the sampling frame at hand. (3) If possible, correct the errors in the list of the population. Each type of error and possible corrective actions are described below.

Non-sampling error

Coverage error

Coverage error occurs when the sampling frame differs systematically from the target population of interest. Sampling frames are generated from available lists, and lists containing accurate and complete information may be difficult to locate or to access. When individuals who are not included on lists differ from the target population in a systematic way, bias is introduced into the study. For example, young people are more likely to have abandoned telephone landlines and instead use only mobile phones. Because directories for mobile phones are not readily available, a random sample drawn from a directory of landline subscribers is likely to be biased toward older users, leaving younger users undercovered. To reduce errors due to undercoverage, two or more lists may be required. However, this may create problems of higher numbers of ineligibles or duplicates, as described below.

Ineligibles

Another source of error in survey research is when people appear in the sampling frame but do not meet the criteria for inclusion in the study. Hence, these individuals are ineligible for inclusion. Other terms for ineligibles are 'foreign elements', 'empty listings', or 'blanks'. For example, in the senior secondary classroom study, there may be a small proportion of adults attending senior secondary classes. If the focus of the study is on people between 17 and 19 years old, adults beyond this age are ineligible for inclusion – including them in the study would bias the results. Because the inclusion of ineligibles will increase the costs and reduce the final sample size of a study, every attempt should be made to screen them out before sampling begins. However, this requires that screening information is available. When it is not possible to screen out ineligibles *a priori*, then an oversampling strategy may be necessary, with screening information included in the survey instrument. In the example above, if age is not available as a screening device, then a question about age should be asked on the survey.

Duplicates or multiplicity

The problem of duplicates arises when the sampling frame contains more than one listing for each element. Duplicates become a problem in that individuals listed more than once have a higher probability of selection in the study. For example, when a master list of health care professionals is compiled from several discrete lists of membership in various health care associations, it is possible that an individual could appear on the master list more than once. Duplicates can be identified and then eliminated by alphabetizing the list and using other criteria (e.g., gender, birth date, mailing address) to determine whether the element is a duplicate.

Clustering

Clustering is the opposite of duplication. It occurs when there is one listing in the sampling frame for several individuals in the population. The most common example of clustering is a single telephone number for more than one member of the household.

Sampling error

Sampling error is simply a mismatch or lack of precision between the selected sample and the population to which the researchers wish to generalize. Because only a proportion of the population is selected for the study, there will always be some slippage between the sample and the population. The goal is to minimize the slippage in order to ensure that the results derived from a sample are representative of the larger population of interest.

In most survey research textbooks, considerable emphasis is placed on the ability to generalize the findings to the larger target population. Hence, sampling error is elevated to the most prominent of all errors encountered in survey research. However, sampling error can only be calculated, and hence is relevant, if the study design is based on a probability sample. The statistics associated with sampling error are based on random sampling, so if they are calculated for studies employing stratified and cluster sampling designs, they will not be accurate.

Moreover, the sampling error can only be calculated on a single variable and not on the complete study. That is, it is not possible to compute a standard error for an entire study, but only on a variable by variable basis.

The calculation of sampling error is based on the rules of probability. Any selected sample of the population will not have properties identical to those of the population. Assuming that the sample has been correctly constructed, drawing multiple smaller random samples from the entire sample and plotting the means of each sample will produce the mean of the sampling distribution, or the *true population mean*. The standard deviation or *standard error* of the true population is the standard deviation of the variable divided by the square root of the number of cases:

$$s_{\bar{x}} = \frac{s_x}{\sqrt{n}}$$

where $s_{\bar{x}}$ is the standard error of the mean, s_x the sample standard deviation of the mean, and n the sample size.

In addition, confidence intervals, which are a range of values within which the true value lies, can be calculated. It is not unusual to read that in a poll of 1500 persons nationwide, 70% of the population favours candidate X over Y with a 95% level of confidence or margin of error of plus or minus 3%. This means that if a complete census of the population were conducted, the true value of the population would be in the range of 67–73%. The lower the standard error and the lower the margin of error, the more confident we are of the results of the study. However, as indicated above, margins of error can be calculated only for individual variables, and hence may vary from variable to variable. Missing data due to item non-response may lead to higher sampling errors for individual variables. For an extended discussion of sampling error, see Ziliak and McCloskey (2008).

Three main factors affect the standard error. First, a larger sample size reduces the standard error as the sample size n is the denominator in the formula. However, there is a limit to the benefits of increasing the sample size. Although the sample size is the denominator of the formula above, the actual value is the square root of the sample size. Hence, doubling the sample size will lower the sampling error somewhat, but will not decrease it by half. Second, smaller variance due to lower heterogeneity of responses to a survey item will result in a smaller standard error. Third, as indicated above, the computation of standard errors by statistical computer packages assumes a simple random sampling design. Standard errors calculated for variables produced from studies employing designs that are not based on simple random sampling will be inaccurate.

It is worth quoting Weisberg (2005: 231) in full regarding sampling error:

> Sampling error is neat to work with since it can be computed mathematically; this makes it seductive to focus on sampling error and ignore the other types of survey error. However, … sampling error is only the tip of the iceberg, and it would be a serious mistake not to take the other sources of error into account in interpreting the results [of a study].

In other words, all of the sources of error identified in this chapter require attention.

Measurement error

Measurement error occurs when a survey item does not measure what it is intended to measure. Often, the survey item is poorly designed, and as a result, respondents are unable to either interpret the item or respond accurately to it. In Chapter 5, survey item design was discussed in detail, with the goal of eliminating measurement error.

Non-response error

Non-response error occurs when individuals who are included in the survey sample do not participate in the study. *Unit-level* response occurs when the individual does not respond to any part of the survey. (*Item-level* non-response is discussed below.) If the unit non-response is systematic, then the study will be biased. Even studies with high response rates may be affected by non-response bias if certain groups are less likely to participate. There are three types of unit non-response: *non-contact*, *incapacity*, and *non-cooperation*.

Non-contact (undeliverable)

Non-contact occurs when it is not possible to locate an individual. Causes of non-contact include invalid mailing addresses and the use of telephone caller ID screening. In these two examples, ensuring that mailing lists are up-to-date and sending out a letter introducing a telephone study may reduce non-contact bias.

Incapacity

Some members of the survey sample may be incapable of participating in the study. Physical or mental illness and lack of ability in the language employed in the study are examples of incapacity. With internet surveys, the inability to manoeuvre internet files is equivalent to incapacity. Non-response due to incapacity is most likely to be random and minimal, unless the target population has a high proportion of one of these groups.

Non-cooperation

In almost all instances, participation in survey research is voluntary. As such, individuals have the right to refuse to participate. Again, if non-cooperation occurs systematically, the results will be biased. Various incentives to participate in survey research projects are described in Chapter 8.

Summary

In this chapter, the interrelated activities of choosing one or more samples through non-probabilistic or probabilistic sampling strategies and assessing and minimizing the multiple sources of error were discussed. I have argued that all sampling strategies begin purposively; that is, the researcher or research team makes judgements about whom to sample, and related issues of how, when, why, and where the sampling process unfolds. Both non-probabilistic and probabilistic sampling strategies are used regularly in survey research. The sampling strategy should be chosen on the basis of best fitting the research questions at hand. Finally, it is imperative to be aware of and document all sources of error related to your research project.

Exercises

1 Describe your sampling strategy in detail. Include descriptions of your frame and target population, intended sample size, and method of sample selection.

2 Describe whether you will employ non-probabilistic, probabilistic sampling strategies, or both, and whether you will use a stratified approach to sampling.

3 Discuss potential non-sampling, sampling, measurement, and non-response errors.

Further reading

Kish, L. (1967). *Survey Sampling*. New York: Wiley.

Weisberg, H. F. (2005). *The Total Survey Error Approach. A Guide to the New Science of Survey Research*. Chicago: University of Chicago Press.

SEVEN

Validity, reliability, and trustworthiness

Validity, goodness, trustworthiness, soundness. These words are used to describe the worth or 'truth value' of a research project. From a survey research perspective, information collected through one or more survey modes is valid or trustworthy to the extent that it (1) produces information that answers the research questions posed by the researcher, (2) accurately describes the sample or population at hand, and, if appropriate, (3) can be extended to individuals beyond the participants of the study.

Each facet of a survey research design – from initial problem formulation to the final response rate – will affect the trustworthiness or validity of the survey research project. Attending to each facet in a thoughtful and informed way will contribute to the truth value of the study.

In this chapter, I review the tenets of validity or soundness and reliability from multiple perspectives in relation to survey research. Quantitative and qualitative research camps have created deep paradigmatic divides regarding these issues. For survey (and other forms of) research, this divide has worsened rather than improved. Rather than arguing the relevance of the criteria specified by one camp over the other, it is more fruitful to consider a broad range of ways of thinking about the topics of validity or goodness with the goal of assessing their usefulness for strengthening a survey research project. I use these terms interchangeably throughout this chapter. Because the term 'survey research' is a rubric for many different modes and methods, and because each component of a multi-method study will have its own unique goodness requirements, different validity criteria for each method may be necessary. It is critical to use the appropriate criteria for the type or types of study or studies undertaken and not adopt blindly criteria designed specifically for experimental or qualitative[2]

---

[2]As I have argued elsewhere in this chapter, much of what is referred to as 'qualitative research' actually falls under the rubric of survey research.

research. What follows is a review and reorganization, from a contemporary perspective, of the classic typology of validity and reliability from a quantitative perspective as presented by Campbell and Stanley (1963), and from a qualitative perspective by Denzin (1989), Guba (1981), Lather (1986), Lincoln and Guba (1985), and Marshall and Rossman (2006) in relation to their relevance for each facet of the various type of survey methods. This chapter is organized under three headings: conceptualizing the study; extending the findings beyond the original study; and threats to the internal validity or soundness of a study.

Conceptualizing the study

Validity or trustworthiness is built into a study from its initial conceptualization. This section should be read together with Chapter 3.

Credibility

As originally specified by Lincoln and Guba (1985), in order for a study to be credible, it must be carried out in a way that ensures that the research participants are described and identified accurately. Every facet described in Chapter 2 is designed to meet this criterion. A full description of each facet, from conceptualization through to data analysis, holds the researcher accountable in ensuring that the study results are an accurate reflection of the participants' behaviours, attitudes, and opinions.

Face validity

In survey research, often the first impression of a questionnaire, related cover letter and other materials will determine whether potential respondents will complete your survey. In the case of interviewer-administered survey research, the appearance, presentation, and performance of the interviewer can affect the face validity of the interview process. Face validity is highly subjective in that, with as little as a single glance, potential respondents can decide to complete your survey, toss it into the recycling bin, delete it from their long list of emails, or tell an interviewer to 'get lost'.

Face validity is often dismissed as superficial and not warranting the attention of the serious scientific researcher. There are no statistical tests to assess face validity (Kidder, 1982). However, the message to be learned by the survey researcher is that first impressions are extremely important. An amateur, sloppy, or dull introductory letter, survey, or both will probably not 'ring true' and hence will not have a long survival period. It is worth the effort to design your survey in a way that will catch the eye of the intended respondent. Relevant content will also enhance the face validity factor. Interviewers who do not act in a professional manner, who appear bored or who are rude will be hung up on or turned away. Chapter 8 provides numerous tips for enhancing the attractiveness of a survey instrument and related contact materials and interviewer-administered surveys.

Content validity

Content validity refers to the relationship of one or more measures to a given construct. In Chapter 3, concepts, latent constructs, and indicator variables were discussed in detail. Clear definitions of constructs should lead to the development of indicators designed to measure that construct. Determination of measures for given constructs relies on a thorough review of the literature, examining previous survey instruments, talking with experts, and piloting questions with individuals similar to the intended sample or population.

In reality, in survey research a handful of constructs will be included on any given instrument. The possibility or probability of measuring all facets of a given construct is small; instead, the research project needs to be delimited to what is reasonably doable in a single survey project. In order to ensure that the content of the survey items are as valid as possible, they should be defined clearly based on rigorous background research. Multiple measures of one construct are desirable and more than one construct with its related measures may be required to capture a multifaceted overarching construct. For example, a construct trying to measure *subjective well-being* may be broken down into the sub-constructs of *overall happiness* and *life satisfaction*. Content validity can be confirmed *ex post facto* through analyses such as factor analysis or structural equation modelling. Also, triangulation of data collection – for example, mail-out surveys and face-to-face interviews – will allow for more in-depth exploration of constructs and related measures.

Construct validity

In Chapter 3, the development of constructs was addressed in great detail. To summarize here, constructs develop from concepts that often start as loosely defined ideas, images, or symbols. Through further specification, a concept is transformed into a construct by specifying its nominal definition and defining its dimensions. Finally, because constructs *per se* are abstract and not directly measurable, concrete measures must be developed that can be used to collect information on a survey instrument.

Content and construct validity go hand-in-hand. Carefully conceptualized constructs without related concrete measures would make survey research impossible to carry out. Concrete measures without carefully defined and crafted constructs may result in the collection of a set of incomplete and disjointed facts.

Criterion validity

To determine the criterion validity of a survey, a set of external criteria or standards is required against which survey results can be compared. However, because surveys are most often comprised of reported behaviours, attitudes, and opinions, assessing the criterion validity of survey results is of limited use. Large-scale surveys, such as those collected along with literacy, mathematics, and science achievement data in the Programme for International Student Achievement (PISA), could be used to compare the results of a local study.

Predictive validity

In survey research, predictive validity refers to the extent to which the measures contained in the survey instrument are able to predict future outcomes. For example, are certain behaviours, attitudes, or opinions reported at one point in time predictive of similar or even dissimilar behaviours, attitudes, or opinions at another point in time? To determine the predictive ability of say, socioeconomic status reported at time 1 on subsequent participation in or completion of university studies at time 2, a panel design (see Chapter 4) would need to be employed. Another approach would be to compare survey data collected at one point in time with other data, for example, university records of participation and completion.

Extending the findings beyond the original study

External validity

External validity is the extent to which the findings of a study of a sample of individuals can be generalized beyond the study sample to its inferential population. The notion of external validity emerged out of experimental research (Campbell and Stanley, 1963), and for much of the twentieth century it was used as the gold standard upon which to judge research. However, as we have seen in Chapter 6, there can be considerable slippage between the target population, the sampling frame, the survey sample, and the actual respondents.

Generalizability is a grandiose goal that aims to take the findings of a single study and assert that the results are applicable to all other individuals, contexts, and temporal periods. Claims of external validity have long been the bane of qualitative, feminist, and post-structuralist researchers who consider such claims as simplistic and not an adequate or accurate description of reality.

Ecological validity

Ecological validity can be considered to be a workable definition of generalizability for the real world. That is, generalizability is usually only realistically attainable when it is delimited to certain contexts, cultures, portions of the population, and temporal periods. In terms of its relevance to survey research, rather than attempting to generalize findings – say, about attitudes toward marijuana use – to an entire universe, we would delimit the generalizability of findings to those who resembled the survey respondents. If the study sample were a sample of 20–25-year-old urban dwellers in the Netherlands, from an ecological perspective, the findings are most plausibly generalizable to the population of young urban adults in the Netherlands. Given differences in laws and attitudes toward marijuana possession and use in different countries, it would not be unexpected to find that young urban adults in the USA or Sweden held different attitudes.

In survey research, we can apply the tenets of ecological validity from initial conception of the study through to the data collection phase. Somehow, however, with a simple sleight of hand, researchers are prone to revert to claims of external validity in order to attempt to convert their carefully delimited study into one that generalizes to a universe that is larger than can be considered credible.

Statistical conclusion validity

The earth is round. (p< .05)

(Cohen, 1994, p. 997)[3]

Statistical conclusion validity requires the use of test statistics to assess the worth of a study. In order to apply the correct test statistics, it is critical to have a sound grasp of statistical theory and its relevant applications in the social sciences. For example, the nature and size of the sample will determine whether and which test statistics can be meaningful employed. As Ziliak and McCloskey (2008) point out, statistics such as Student's t or p-values that were developed to determine

---

[3] I use this quote as Ziliak and McCloskey (2008) *The Cult of Statistical Significance: How the Standard Error Costs Us Jobs, Justice, and Lives.* Ann Arbor: The University of Michigan press do.

sampling precision – that is, the statistical significance of a sample – are frequently misused to make claims about the significance of the findings in relation to theory and related hypotheses. Instead, they argue, we as researchers should be focusing on the 'oomph' value of our studies. To do this, they assert that we should be using indicators of significance that address issues of '*how much* and *who cares?*'. To determine the latter requires the reporting of descriptive statistics, including all relevant variables in analyses, conducting exploratory analyses, reporting negative results, taking into account other sources of error in a study (see Chapter 6), calculating power and related effect sizes, reporting confidence intervals, employing a multi-method approach to research, and replicating studies (Cohen, 1994; Ziliak and McCloskey, 2008).

Numerical data gathered through survey research methods are conducive to quantitative analyses. However, incorrect use of statistical techniques does not in any way demonstrate that the findings are valid.

Substantive validity

In order to address the substantive significance of findings, answers to the questions '*how much* and *who cares?*' (Ziliak and McCloskey, 2008) must be provided. Researchers who are interested in the substantive impact of their research use statistic inference techniques, at most and only when appropriate, as only one small indicator of 'the size and importance of relationships' (2008: 2) and will instead employ many of the techniques listed above to determine the sociological, economic, medical, pharmaceutical, or other disciplinary significance on people's lives. In Chapter 1, I summarized how Charles Booth conducted 'surveys' with the goal of both understanding and changing the plight of London's poor population. The occupational focus of William Gosset, statistician, head experimental brewer at the Guinness Brewery from 1907 to 1935, and creator of the Student's *t* test statistic, was to determine the extent to which the results of research conducted should be used to change brewing practices that would enhance customer satisfaction without unduly increasing costs to the company. In other words, from a business perspective, the substantive significance for Gosset rested in the bottom line.

Recently published research on survey research can be scrutinized for its substantive significance. For example, a study by Galesic and Bosnjak (2009) sought to determine the effect of questionnaire length on completion rates of web surveys. Volunteers responding to web banners were randomly assigned into one of the following three groups where the introductory page indicated that the survey would take 10, 20, or 30 minutes to complete. All groups were able, but not required, to complete the entire survey (i.e., the 30-minute version). Although the researchers demonstrated statistical significance in several ways, findings that could have been used to demonstrate substantive significance were largely buried in tables and were not included in the discussion section. As a survey researcher, I am interested in the finding that only 327 of the 3472 respondents completed the entire survey (assigned and additional) and that 9% of the 10-minute, 8% of the 20-minute, and 11% of the 30-minute group did so. These are substantive findings that would help me make decisions about survey length. In other words, 'the major emphasis should be on the substantive meaningfulness of the findings' (Pedhazur, 1982).

In another recent study, Holland and Christian (2008) surveyed 13,391 university students to determine the effectiveness of probing in open-ended web surveys. The response rate – a startlingly low 9% – is mentioned only briefly and never addressed as a substantive concern in terms of the substantive significance of the study.

Substantive validity, which embraces the plain-English definition of 'significant', is a necessary component of any survey research project. As the famous statistician John Tukey (1969: 90) concluded in his invited address to the American Psychological Association, 'data analysis has its major uses. They are detective work and guidance counseling. Let us all try to act accordingly'.

Transferability

By employing the notion of transferability, the onus for demonstrating generalizability is shifted away from the researcher and her/his related findings and toward those who wish to partly or fully replicate the study. The researchers who are interested in replicating some or all of the study are responsible for assessing the extent to which the research questions, design, sample, method(s) of administration, findings, and implications for further research are useful for the new study being contemplated (Lincoln and Guba, 1985; Marshall and Rossman, 2006). Good research always engages in some form of transferability. Through a rigorous review of the literature, each of the components of existing related studies is assessed for its relevance to the new study being considered.

Catalytic validity

The term 'catalytic validity' was coined for use in 'openly ideological research' (Lather, 1986). The goal of this type of research is to enlighten participants regarding the reality of their situations in order to empower them to transform certain aspects of their lives. Rather than treating research participants as objects and hence 'targets of research' (Lather, 1986), it considers them to be actively engaged participants to the point that, through the process of participating in a research study, they gain knowledge about, and perhaps the skills to change their life situations.

At first glance, the idea of catalytic validity may seem irrelevant to survey research. However, ethics guidelines are shifting in ways that support and encourage engagement, empowerment, and self-determination on the part of those who participate in research. More and more, we as researchers are being asked to account for the extent to which our research benefits the communities in which it is being conducted. That is, rather than just 'taking' from participants their time and energy, we are increasingly expected to 'give back' in the form of community engagement and capacity building. Even shifts in terminology signal that power relationships between the researchers and the researched are identified with the goal of rebalancing previous imbalances. For example, according to the Canadian Institutes of Health Research, Natural Sciences and Engineering Research Council of Canada, from an ethics policy perspective, the term 'participant' is preferred to 'subjects' 'because it better reflects the spirit behind the core principles [of ethical conduct]; that individuals who choose to participate in research play a more active role than the term "subject" conveys' (Canadian Institutes of Health Research et al., 2010: 16).

Also, research for the twenty-first century should be designed in a way that is relevant to a given community by incorporating its needs and priorities (Canadian Institutes of Health Research et al., 2010). Some communities, such as the indigenous peoples of Canada and New Zealand, have taken charge of whether, how, and under what conditions research occurs. Decades or even centuries of being treated as research 'objects' has resulted in the view that the word '"research" is probably one of the dirtiest words in the indigenous world's vocabulary' (Smith, 1999). Guidelines such as those that appear in contemporary codes of ethics (e.g., Canadian Institutes of Health Research et al., 2010) contain sections that address the unique nature of conducting research with indigenous communities. All researchers can learn from those who write about respect, relevance, reciprocity, and responsibility (Kirkness and Barnhardt, 1991) in relation to research activity.

Throughout this text, I have argued that survey research is not and cannot be objective and neutral. The degree to which survey research can be openly ideological spans from minimal to maximal. 'Fugging' – 'fundraising under the guise of a survey' (Weisberg, 2005: 35) – is a blatant attempt to legitimize the transmission of openly ideological messages by employing survey research techniques (see Chapter 5 for examples). Minimally, a survey research project may raise the awareness levels of participants on certain topics or issues. Each facet of the survey research process as described in Chapter 2 will be more or less ideological in its orientation.

Reliability

Reliability refers to the extent to which the findings of a study can be replicated. Again, the term has been adapted from research conducted under experimental conditions in a laboratory setting. But what does it mean for the survey researcher?

First, the measures contained in the survey instrument must be designed in a clear and unambiguous way to ensure that the respondent would answer the item in the same way if s/he were asked to repeat the exercise. Because most survey research is not conducted under experimental conditions, this is a hypothetical requirement. Demonstrating reliability of responses does not mean that the survey items are valid. For instance, a survey item intended to be a measure of overall happiness may indeed measure something else. But if respondents gave the same answer to the question asked at different time periods (but keeping everything else constant), the item would be considered to be reliable. Like the gas or petrol gauge in an automobile, when the level of gas or petrol is reduced to a certain level, the needle will always register that the tank is empty. However, this information may or may not be valid; indeed, it may be possible to travel another 20–50 kilometres on this 'empty' tank!

Reliability also means the extent to which a study can be replicated with similar samples and in similar conditions to produce similar results. Because the social world is messy, exact replication of the results of a survey research project is highly unlikely. But if similar trends in the findings can be determined, the measures and methods employed can be considered to be reliable.

Threats to the internal validity or soundness of a study

The tenets of internal validity were specified by Campbell and Stanley (1963) to determine whether the effects of an experiment were indeed caused by the experiment and not by other rival factors. These criteria are often employed or adapted to assess the internal validity of other forms of research. Qualitative researchers have reworked, extended, and to some extent invented new criteria of soundness or trustworthiness of a study (Lincoln and Guba, 1985; Marshall and Rossman, 2006).

Campbell and Stanley (1963) insisted that the single best way to control threats to internal validity is through randomization of the sample. However, as I have discussed at great length in Chapter 6, randomization is often either not possible, not desirable, or both in survey research. This does not mean, however, that some of Campbell and Stanley's original specifications are not useful. They, along with the criteria of soundness or trustworthiness in the qualitative research literature, need to be reworked to be suitable for a survey research project. Rather than trying to separate 'effects' from 'rival causes' in survey research, it is more reasonable to ask whether there are factors external to the purpose and design of the study that could explain the results. The threats to internal validity are considered in this section under the headings generated by Campbell and Stanley and related terms generated by others.

History or dependability

According to Campbell and Stanley (1963), specific events outside the control of an experiment could adversely affect the results. To control for the effect of *history*, participants in experiments are sequestered to ensure that events do not taint data collection. In survey research, events may indeed affect the outcomes of a study. If the data collection phase of a survey project was under way between 1 September and 30 September 2001, the events of 11 September would indeed have some impact on the response rate and responses before and after this fateful date. The Japanese earthquake of 11 March 2011 and the ensuing tsunami would have had a profound impact on the results of a survey under way at the time of its occurrence. One way to control for events external to a survey research study is to collect the data in a very short time period. For example, during an election campaign, pollsters collect data via telephone within a very short window of time, for example between 6 p.m. and 9 p.m. on a given day, in order to control for the effects of, say, the late night news, gaffes by politicians, or the release of other polling results. In projects where surveys are administered, completed, and returned over a longer period of time, it is beyond the ability of the survey researcher to control for external events.

Qualitative researchers use the term *dependability* to account for changing conditions as a result of history. Rather than attempting to control for these effects, the effects of history are described in detail in the research methods, findings, and discussion sections of reports emerging from research projects.

The survey researcher needs to be aware of the impact of history on the results of a study. The extent to which controls should be imposed or the extent to which events will be accounted for will depend on the purpose, sample(s), and mode(s) of data collection.

Maturation

Over time, the intra-individual characteristics of respondents change. They may become hungry or tired, and as a result, their interest in completing a mail or web survey or a face-to-face or telephone interview may change from enthusiasm to boredom. The greater the period of time involved in data collection, the greater the potential effect of maturation; for example, the sample will grow older. Survey researchers employing interviewer-administered methods, in particular, need to be aware of the demands they impose on their volunteer participants. The research literature suggests that if the instrument is too long, respondents will answer questions – particularly open-ended questions – more hastily and inattentively (Stern et al., 2007). In an experimental study to determine, in part, response patterns in relation to questionnaire length in web surveys, Galesic and Bosnjak (2009) randomized the order of blocks of questions. Their findings demonstrated that the average variance of responses to questions that appeared further from the beginning of the questionnaire decreased. Also, respondents spent less time answering questions closer to the end than at the beginning of the survey. To assess whether this study and its related sample and recruitment method (e.g., volunteers responding to banner advertisements) is credible, it is important to read the entire study. In addition, the authors acknowledge that another potential internal validity – a learning effect – may account for the latter finding (see the subsection below on 'testing').

Instrumentation

The survey instrument itself may affect the results of a study. In panel studies, changes to the instrumentation may be the cause of changes in responses between data collected at earlier and subsequent time points. For instance, by simply changing the wording of the five-point scale in Example 7.1 to that contained in Example 7.2, different responses may result.

Example 7.1 Rating Scale 1

| Not at all important | Not very important | No opinion | Somewhat important | Very important |

Example 7.2 Rating Scale 2

| Not at all important | Not very important | Neither important nor unimportant | Somewhat important | Very important |

With interviewer-administered surveys that are intended to be tightly scripted, a subtle change in wording, tone, or inflection to a question can affect responses (Dillman, 2000). To curtail the effects of instrumentation, the researcher must weigh the purpose of the survey with the mode of administration.

Testing

Testing emerges as an internal threat to validity when the effects of taking an initial test affect the results of a second test. In survey research, we do not conduct 'tests'; however, in panel designs, participation in an initial phase of a study may affect responses – and perhaps even behaviours – in subsequent phases. During the second follow-up interview in my longitudinal research with Grade 12 students in May 1990, I asked them if having participated in the first interview in November 1989 had made any difference in their lives. Almost all of them replied that the questions I had asked – about whether they planned to continue on to post-secondary education; if so, what type of institution; and (3) to explain their answers to these questions – had raised their sensitivity about the choices available and how they were (mis)informed about their options and attitudes. Did participation in this research project at age 18 affect their subsequent post-secondary behaviour?

Also, the notion of test effects may take the form of learning effects in survey research. In the study by Galesic and Bosnjak (2009) described above, the researchers conceded that the finding that respondents spent less time answering questions that were positioned at the end of the study than those appearing at the beginning may have been due to learning. That is, during the course of completing a 30-minute web survey, it was possible that respondents 'learned' how to respond more quickly to survey items as they progressed through the survey.

Selection

When conducting comparative studies, it is possible to build in biases through different selection processes for the comparison groups. For example, international comparative studies of post-secondary participation can be highly problematic due to: the varying definitions of 'post-secondary'; varying access to different groups of students due to ethics requirements or country-specific mores; or the proclivity of certain countries to permit access to only their high-achieving students.

TEXT BOX 7.1

International comparative research

The threat of selection may be exacerbated in international comparative research.

Pre-emptive measures include having a detailed understanding of the populations at hand and establishing clear definitions for selection rules. If possible and desirable, some form of random selection of groups can be carried out.

Mortality

In survey research, mortality or attrition is a non-sampling error. The most carefully crafted sample can be undermined by non-response rates in certain groups. When moderating variables such as gender are used to form comparative groups, biases from lower response rates by men (typical in survey research) will bias the results. Oversampling those who may be less likely to participate (see Chapter 6) as well as rigorous follow-up of non-respondents (see Chapter 8) may reduce sample mortality.

Statistical regression

Campbell and Stanley (1963) define this threat as 'groups [that] have been selected on the basis of their extreme scores' on a pretest. As such, in subsequent testing, their responses will be closer to the mean. This threat is not particularly relevant to survey research.

Confirmability

The criterion of confirmability has been developed for its application to qualitative research. Because its goal is to provide a set of checks against the introduction of bias of interpretation, it is instructive to consider some of these checks in relation to all of the modes of survey research and not only data collected through interviews. Here, I use five of the seven criteria specified by Marshall and Rossman (2006) in modified form as suitable for survey research.

The first check specifies that one or more individuals adopt the role of 'devil's advocate' by interrogating the analyses employed by the researcher. In other words, a different set of eyes may be able to detect biases embedded in the analysis that are not obvious to the principal researcher. Second, Marshall and Rossman's suggestion that negative instances in the data should be sought can be augmented by employing the three purposes of triangulation as specified by Mathison (1988): convergence, inconsistency, and contradiction (see Chapters 2 and 3 above for a more in-depth discussion). The third check involves the inclusion of rival hypotheses in order to strengthen the integrity of the findings. Fourth, note-taking practices on the part of the researcher help to provide memory cues of certain events that occurred during the course of the study and can help with the interpretation. The final check is that of an audit; in doing so, the researcher assesses her/his own background, perceptions, and interests in relation to the data collection process and analyses.

Summary

In this chapter, I have reviewed issues of validity, reliability, and trustworthiness with the goal of assessing the truth value of a study. The multifaceted nature of survey research does not lend itself to one approach. Instead, survey researchers need to be familiar with the different ways of assessing validity, reliability, and trustworthiness and engage in research practices that ensure that the findings are rigorous.

Exercises

1 Make a list of the headings (e.g., catalytic validity, history or dependability) included in the chapter. Generate notes under each heading regarding the role this dimension plays in your study.

2 What actions do you need to take to ensure the 'truth value' of your research findings?

Further reading

Campbell, D. T., and Stanley, J. C. (1963) *Experimental and Quasi-experimental Designs for Research.* Dallas: Houghton Mifflin.

Lather, P. (1986) Issues of validity in openly ideological research: Between a rock and a soft place. *Interchange,* 17(4), 63–84.

Lincoln, Y. S., and Guba, E. (1985) *Naturalistic Inquiry.* Beverly Hills, CA: Sage.

Marshall, C., and Rossman, G. B. (2006) *Designing Qualitative Research.* Thousand Oaks, CA: Sage.

Ziliak, S. T., and McCloskey, D. N. (2008) *The Cult of Statistical Significance: How the Standard Error Costs Us Jobs, Justice, and Lives.* Ann Arbor: University of Michigan Press.

EIGHT

Administration of surveys and enhancing response rates

Ensuring high response rates is key in any survey research project. In this chapter, a comprehensive description of how to enhance response rates is provided, beginning with the initial conceptualization of the study through to multiple follow-ups. Issues of ethics are highlighted throughout the chapter, for example, in relation to the voluntary nature of participation, the use of incentives, and following-up with non-respondents.

This chapter includes a detailed account of how to prepare pre-contact materials (e.g., letters of introduction, consent forms, and reminder cards), and a discussion of the use of incentives, the frequency, timing and types of follow-ups, and other techniques to prevent or reduce non-response. In addition, the need to train research and project assistants is reinforced.

In the previous chapters, the facets presented in Figure 2.1 were portrayed with the goal of ultimately enhancing response rates. At this point, we have considered the following: careful identification of the research problem and related questions; locating yourself in the study and anticipating your audience; using triangulation to determine what is already known; considering the ethical implications of every facet of survey design; determining what skills you will need to be an effective survey researcher; thoughtful specification of the survey sample and choice of one or more survey instruments suitable for the nature of the study and the sample; and designing the survey instrument. Careful attention to each of these facets will help you to achieve high response rates. However, there are several specific techniques and strategies with which survey researchers engage before, during, and after the administration of surveys that will enhance survey responses even more. These techniques and strategies will be considered under three headings: the survey package, incentives, and follow-ups.

In each of the steps that precede survey administration, the need for attention to detail has been highlighted. This attention must continue throughout the process of administering your survey instrument. In addition, evidence of a 'personal touch' will demonstrate to potential respondents that the study is important, that you as the researcher are actively engaged in the survey process, and that you are willing to give your time and energy in exchange for your respondents' time and energy.

In this phase of your survey research, you must have a detailed plan for administration, and you must ensure that this plan is followed. The plan includes the date for initial survey administration and the frequency and timing of follow-ups. Also, you must anticipate any potential timing problems. For example, the beginning and end of each academic term in elementary and secondary schools is not a good choice for administering surveys. Each sample will have its own unique monthly, quarterly, or yearly rhythm. It is essential to familiarize yourself with the characteristics of your sample in order to ensure that the timing of initial survey administration and subsequent mail-outs will work in favour of, and not against, enhancing response rates.

In addition, unless respondents agree to be associated with their responses, anonymity of responses must be ensured. It is important to make the distinction between confidentiality and anonymity. Often, researchers mistakenly guarantee that all responses will be confidential. If that were the case, none of the findings of the study could be reported! What the researchers mean to say is that personal information will remain confidential; as a result, anonymity of responses is ensured.

TEXT BOX 8.1

Ethics Alert!

The University of British Columbia Behavioural Review of Ethics Guidance Notes provide clear definitions of anonymity and confidentiality:

Anonymity: The research subject is only anonymous if the data does not include any identifiers, codes, or unique information that can be used to identify the subject. If the subject has participated in a face-to-face interview, he/she is not anonymous. On the other hand, the data may be anonymous if someone other than the researchers have removed all identifiers from the data, or the key linking the subject to code numbers or pseudonyms is destroyed.

A subject might be said to be anonymous: a) as the result of database linkages, where the researcher receives anonymous data only, or b) if the subject is completing a questionnaire that requires absolutely no identifying information, and he/she has not been recruited because of membership in a group whose membership is so restricted, unusual, prominent, or otherwise

---

individually identifiable, that particular members can be identified even without specific information within (or attached to) their data.

It is usually more appropriate to promise confidentiality to a subject, than to promise anonymity.

Confidentiality: The raw data may include the name and/or other identifiers, such as a code or membership in a group, which can be used to link the data to the subject's name. The research team will have access to this information, but it will not be included in the final reports of the research, nor will anyone other than those specified in the consent form be given access to the data. If subjects wish to have their comments attributed, this should be specified in the consent form.

Source: http://rise.ubc.ca/helpCenter/GN/BREB_Guidance_Notes.html

Check your institution's ethical review board requirements for survey research.

Each institution and related national granting agency organizations in a given jurisdiction will have its own set of guidelines which must be consulted before you commence your research. Also, research undertaken in more than one country must abide by all the relevant ethics guidelines.

Budget and survey schedule

Before embarking on your survey research project, a carefully crafted and 'doable' budget and schedule should be devised. The funds that you have at your disposal may well determine the scope and extent of your survey research project. In Example 8.1, I provide an example of a budget for a mixed methods survey research project entailing both a mail-out survey and face-to-face interviews. Each cost-related item is documented. In Example 8.2, a schedule for this research project is presented.

The survey package

The survey instrument is only one part of the 'survey package'. The contents of the package will vary by mode of delivery and will determine whether certain requirements, such as those imposed by post-secondary institution ethics boards, must be included. The survey package may contain each of the following: a cover letter and related follow-up letters, a consent form, outgoing envelope, return envelope, incentive and other enclosures, and follow-up postcards.

Example 8.1   Budget

1. Questionnaires and interviews	$
Survey questionnaire	
Cost of printing questionnaire, envelopes, cover letter, reminder postcard, and follow-up letter...	3500
Postage costs for questionnaire (based on the 2011 business reply return fee schedule and postage rates)	
Business Reply Mail (BRM) annual permit..	575
Postage (outgoing & return) for mail-out of survey questionnaires (x 2) and postcard reminder (based on initial sample of 733 questionnaires and business reply return)..	3900
Telephone follow-up and administration of a short questionnaire of non-respondents (based on 200 non-respondents x 45 min. x .15/min.)...................................	1350
Follow-up interviews	
Travel to interview locations	6000
accommodation (20 nights @ $100/night)...........................$2000	
subsistence (20 days @ $50/day)... $1000	
air travel/car rental..$3000	
Other supplies	
Telephone ($200 long distance), fax ($100), courier ($175), photocopying ($500), misc. supplies ($125), memory sticks/ external hard drive ($200)...	1300
2. Other expenses	
Transcription of interview tapes ($100 per hour of tape)	
2.0 hours x 30 interviews x $100 + GST...	6420
3. Non-disposable equipment	
Equipment	
Equipment required for follow-up interviews (tape recorder, microphone audio, tapes)...	300
Computer software	
Software (SPSS annual UBC site license fees; Atlasti software)...	1600
TOTAL	**24,945**

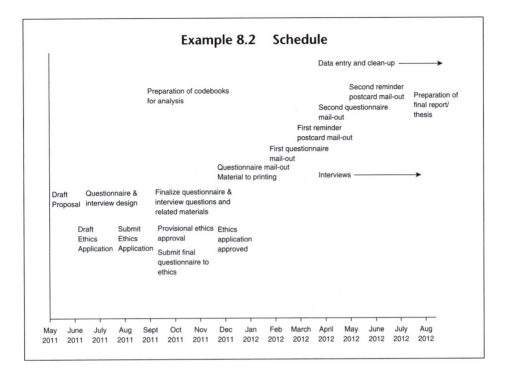

Example 8.2   Schedule

Data entry and clean-up →

Preparation of codebooks for analysis

Second reminder postcard mail-out

Second questionnaire mail-out

Preparation of final report/ thesis

First reminder postcard mail-out

First questionnaire mail-out

Questionnaire mail-out Material to printing

Interviews →

Draft Proposal

Questionnaire & interview design

Finalize questionnaire & interview questions and related materials

Draft Ethics Application

Submit Ethics Application

Provisional ethics approval

Submit final questionnaire to ethics

Ethics application approved

May 2011 | June 2011 | July 2011 | Aug 2011 | Sept 2011 | Oct 2011 | Nov 2011 | Dec 2011 | Jan 2012 | Feb 2012 | March 2012 | April 2012 | May 2012 | June 2012 | July 2012 | Aug 2012

The survey package should be as personalized as possible. Handwritten salutations and signatures indicate to respondents that the researcher has taken the time to address them personally. In my longitudinal research project, I have always personalized the salutation and signed cover letters and reminder postcards. Even when the mail-outs were in the thousands, I maintained that a personal touch on my part would bode well in terms of response rates. In this chapter, I use examples from my longitudinal study. These examples have been modified to represent a current, rather than panel, study.

Cover letters

Cover letters are intended to introduce the survey research project to a given sample of respondents and to invite them to participate in the study. A cover letter may accompany the survey instrument in the case of a mail survey, or have embedded within it the web link and access codes for an online survey.

For telephone and face-to-face surveys, cover letters are mailed in advance. Ethical review boards may have requirements prohibiting 'cold call' telephone contact to individuals. Instead, it may be necessary to make the initial contact through email or mail contact.

Some texts on survey research (e.g., Dillman, 2000) make a strong argument for the practice of always sending out a pre-notice letter one week in advance of the survey instrument. Given that each survey situation is somewhat unique, the practice of always sending an initial letter must be weighed against the cost, which will be considerable in large-scale mail surveys, and the potential of annoying potential respondents through unnecessary email messages for web surveys.

The cover letter should be designed to appeal to your research sample. Although all cover letters must contain certain elements, their order may vary depending on the audience. Different countries have their own protocols for letter construction; when conducting international comparative research, it is strongly advised to work with someone whose first language is spoken in the country or countries engaged in the research.

Also, the choice of font should correspond to the characteristics of the audience. Whereas a more playful font could be used with a younger audience of adolescents or young adults, a more sombre font may be more appropriate for a professional audience. Word-processing programs and survey web design programs are replete with font choices, and the choice you make will change the texture of your cover letter, as will good-quality paper. Example 8.3 shows some of the fonts available in Microsoft Word.

Example 8.3   Font types

CHALKDUSTER	PLAYFUL, YOUTHFUL
Apple Chancery	artistic
Garamond	legal, official
Arial Narrow	neutral, efficient

The font size should be adjusted to be easily readable by your sample. For example, the font size should be larger to accommodate for the diminished ability of an older sample of individuals to read fine print.

Figure 8.1 contains a sample cover letter to be mailed to respondents. A cover letter should usually be no longer than one page in length and may contain some or all of the following elements highlighted below.

Date

It is common practice in both personal and business transactions to include a date in a letter. It provides the recipient with a temporal point of reference. With web surveys, initial contact by email will be dated automatically.

Heading

The heading contains your mailing address. Also, it may contain your telephone and fax numbers and email address. If institutional printed or engraved stationary is available, it should be used (and may be required by institutional ethics boards) to add an air of legitimacy and authority to your study. On hard-copy letters, the heading is placed on the right-hand side of the letter. In email based correspondence, the heading is usually placed in the signature.

Inside address

The inside address contains the name, address, and postal code of the survey respondent. It is placed on the left-hand side of a hard-copy letter. In email correspondence, the email address serves the purpose of an inside address.

Salutation

Also called the complimentary address, the salutation must be chosen very carefully. Conventions will vary by age groups, countries, and language groups. In North America, there is a tendency to be less formal and it is not unusual to address individuals by their first names. In other cultures, for example the German-speaking world, it would be considered impolite to address individuals other than family or close friends by their first names. Following conventions is equally important with email correspondence. Employing an improper salutation in either a hard-copy letter or an email may have a negative effect on your response rates.

Salutations can be generated electronically or can be handwritten. If appropriate, a hard-copy cover letter can be personalized by crossing out the printed name and handwriting a name. In my 22-year longitudinal research project, I have always personalized the salutations of my respondents as depicted in Figure 8.1.

Body

The body of the letter should contain several components: a paragraph explaining the purpose of the study; details about you as the researcher; instructions for completing the survey; a paragraph specifying ethical details related to participation in the study and subsequent use of the data; and a closing paragraph. Below is a suggested, but not mandatory, paragraph order that corresponds to Figure 8.1.

The first paragraph should pique the respondent's interest. Starting a cover letter with the opening sentence, 'My name is Jill Jack and I am conducting a survey as part of my doctoral degree' is dull and unengaging. Instead, the opening line

a place of mind
THE UNIVERSITY OF BRITISH COLUMBIA

Department of Educational Studies
Faculty of Education
2125 Main Mall
Vancouver, B.C. Canada V6T 1Z4

May 28, 2011

Tel: 604-822-5374
Fax: 604-822-4244
Web: http://www.edst.educ.ubc.ca

> Hand written salutation

Dear 1988 ~~Grade 12 Graduate~~, *Sarah,*

You are part of an important and unique new study of British Columbia young adults called the **Paths on Life's Way Project**. In this study, I am interested in learning about your educational, work, and life plans following high school graduation. I am inviting you to participate in a survey, **Class of 2011, Life After High School.** This survey is being sent to a sample of the 2011 British Columbia graduating class.

This study is the **only** study of its kind in British Columbia and will continue to greatly extend our knowledge about the educational, work, family, and other experiences of B.C. young adults. Individuals at all stages of their lives may benefit from the results of this research. Information is available on the **Paths** research web site http://www.edst.educ.ubc.ca/paths/paths.htm.

I hope that you will take approximately 45 minutes to respond to this survey. Please return the questionnaire in the enclosed self-addressed stamped envelope as soon as possible. As a 2011 British Columbia Grade 12 graduate, you are the *only* source of this valuable information. I therefore request your patience in answering these questions honestly and carefully. The opinions of everyone receiving the survey are important to the study.

Your participation is voluntary and there are no consequences for choosing not to participate. Please note that your name, signature, or identification are **NOT** required. Only my research assistants and I will have access to the data for coding and analytical purposes. Identification numbers are used for statistical purposes only. Data from all phases of this study will be analyzed by me, together with my students and colleagues, for long term trends. You will **NEVER** be identified by name in reports and publications resulting from this study.

Also find enclosed our latest research report on this project and a small token of appreciation for participating in this study. The research report is also available on the **Paths** web site.

Thank you for participating in this survey. If you have any questions, please call Dr. Lesley Andres at **(604) 822-8943** or by fax **(604) 822-4244** or email **lesley.andres@ubc.ca.** If you have any concerns about this study, please contact the Director of the UBC Office of Research Services and Administration, at 604-822-8598.

Yours sincerely,

Lesley

> Hand written signature

> Customized logo design for the study

Lesley Andres
Professor

Figure 8.1 Cover letter

should begin with something about the study that is compelling. A second short paragraph can expand on the first paragraph in order to explain why the research is important, and how the results will be used to inform practice, policy, research, and/or theory.

If your identity is unknown to your respondents, the next paragraph can contain details about you as the researcher. Your name, position, and your involvement in the study can be included here.

The next paragraph should provide instructions for completing the survey. This paragraph may contain an accurate estimation of how long it will take to complete the survey and return instructions. Inclusion of a 'complete the survey by <date>' is not recommended, unless the timeliness of responses is critical to the purpose of the survey. Respondents who have not completed the survey by the date you have specified will assume that their response is no longer wanted. As a result, responses rates will be negatively affected.

For web surveys, instructions for logging on with PINs and passwords must be provided. Also, the URL hyperlink required to gain access to the survey must be embedded in the text of the email.

The next paragraph should provide details about ethical considerations – both those required by ethic boards and those that should be part of any research project. The voluntary nature of the survey and the right to refuse to answer questions or withdraw at any time should be clearly specified. Contact information for institutional ethics boards may be required. Also, a statement about how the responses will be used may be necessary. The guarantee of anonymity of responses, if accurate, should be specified. If survey identification numbers are affixed to instruments, they must be explained.

Any information that will be linked with the survey data, but not provided directly by respondents, must be disclosed in the cover letter. Grades earned at schools or post-secondary institutions or information from medical records are examples. In order to obtain and use these types of information, formal consent may be required (see the section on consent, below). A statement about incentives, and other enclosures, should be included in the cover letter as a free-standing paragraph or as part of another paragraph.

The closing paragraph provides an opportunity to thank respondents in advance for their participation. Also, respondents should be invited to contact the researcher with any concerns or questions. Additional contact information, such as telephone numbers and email addresses, can be provided.

The complimentary close

In English, there are several options for closing a letter. Common complimentary closes are 'Yours truly', 'Sincerely', and 'Sincerely yours'. The choice of complimentary close is a matter of individual taste and tone. With adults, it is usually better to err on the side of formality. Other languages have their own conventions which should be followed in international comparative research.

Unless it is not feasible, the letter should be signed by hand. Thousands of letters can be signed in less than one hour (something I do often while attending meetings!). This detail adds a personal touch and shows that you are willing to make an effort to ensure a high response rate.

Logo

A logo designed specifically for the survey serves to provide a personal touch and creates a recognizable visual aid to help respondents associate contact material with the study. Logos can be designed by graphic artists. Also, tools in word-processing or publishing programs on today's computers can be used to produce a cost-effective logo.

Comments about formatting

Cover letters should be designed according to the conventions of a business letter. Formatting such as bold, italics, underlining, or combinations of these should be used judiciously. Overuse of formatting results in a cluttered appearance which defeats, rather than enhances, the attempt to place emphasis on important words or phrases in the letter. 'Suggs' and 'fuggs' as described in Chapter 6 are notorious for the overuse of formatting.

Cover letters should be printed on high-quality paper such as institutional letterhead or 24 pound (100 gsm) bond paper with a watermark. Neutral colours such as white or off-white are usually preferable to coloured paper.

Outgoing and return envelopes

To enhance the attractiveness of outgoing and return envelopes for mail surveys, they can be personalized with logos that are preferably printed on the envelopes. Customized envelopes can be produced by a printing shop or, for small-scale surveys, with a laserjet colour printer.

Postage on outgoing envelopes is an obvious requirement. In order to enhance response rates, it is imperative to provide postage on return envelopes. With large mail-outs, it may be more cost-effective to use business-reply postage (or its equivalent, which will vary by country) which is printed onto the envelope. Whether business-reply postage is cost-effective will depend on the sample size and the frequency of mail follow-ups. It is advisable to consult with a postal representative to determine whether business-reply post-age and related administrative fees and minimum mail-out numbers are feasible and cost-effective options. Since postage services vary by country, procedural details are not provided here. Also, postal rules and regulations change over time. For a more detailed account of Canadian postal services, see Guppy and Gray (2008). Dillman (2000) offers an extended discussion of US postal service protocols.

When stamps are used, it is worth the effort to peruse postal service catalogues to choose an attractive stamp. If large quantities of stamps are required, it may be necessary order them in advance.

Mailing labels with the names and addresses of respondents can be produced from databases with the aid of 'mail merge' tools in word-processors. Labels are affixed to the outgoing envelope. An efficient way to prepare for follow-ups is to produce several sets of mail labels. The first set is used for the initial mail-out. As surveys are returned, the labels on the remaining sets are crossed out. When it is time to conduct the next survey mail-out, those that have not been crossed out are affixed to reminder cards or a subsequent survey mail-out package.

It is important to indicate on the outgoing envelope that, in the case of unde-liverable outgoing survey packages, they are to be returned to the sender. In Canada, the phrase 'Return Requested' signals to the postal agent that envelopes with invalid postal addresses will be returned to the sender.

Research on survey mail-outs indicates strongly that stamps rather than metered post should be affixed to return envelopes (Dillman, 2000). Again, it is worth the effort to chose an attractive stamp. However, in the case where some respondents live outside the country from which the survey is being adminis-tered, it is not possible to provide return postage. It is important to acknowledge to respondents that you are aware of this fact. Instead, some other token can be offered. In the 22-year follow-up of my longitudinal project, I purchased beauti-ful 'Year of the Tiger' stamps that I sent as a gift to my respondents living abroad, in lieu of return postage. A handwritten note accompanied the commemorative stamp. It goes without saying that return envelopes must be pre-printed with return addresses.

Reminder postcards

Reminder postcards, either physical or virtual, should be sent at one or more points in time during the course of survey administration. They can serve two pur-poses: thanking those who have completed the survey, and a gentle reminder to those who have not yet done so. Procedures for survey follow-up are highlighted later in this chapter. Here, the contents of the reminder are specified. Figure 8.2 is an example of a postal reminder card. In the first paragraph, the respondent is informed that a survey was sent to her/him two weeks ago. The second paragraph thanks those who have already completed and returned the survey. The third paragraph invites those who have not returned surveys to do so. Finally, contact information for the researcher is supplied. In all of my survey research projects, I have hand-signed the reminder postcards.

Class of 2011, Life After High School

Two weeks ago, I requested your participation in a new study about your educational, work, and life plans following high school graduation. This study is the only study of its kind in British Columbia. Your response is very important to the overall value of the study.

If you have already completed and returned the questionnaire *entitled **Class of 2011, Life After High School,*** please accept my sincere thanks. If not, I ask that you take a few minutes now to do so.

If you have not received a questionnaire, or it has been misplaced, please call me at (604) 822-8943, or contact me by fax (604) 822-4244 or email at **lesley.andres@ubc.ca** and I will ensure that you receive another questionnaire.

Your assistance is very much appreciated.

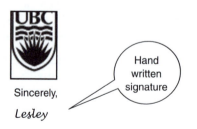

Lesley Andres
Professor, University of British Columbia
Paths on Life's Way Website: http://www.edst.educ.ubc.ca/paths/paths.htm

Figure 8.2 Reminder postcard

Reminder postcards can be produced by printing shops. A cost-effective alternative is to buy unlined recipe cards and create the postcard with a laser printer.

Consent forms

Research conducted by individuals employed by or studying at institutions such as universities, hospitals, and schools will be subject to approval by institutional ethical review boards. Through the completion of ethics applications, the type and nature of consent(s) required will become apparent. Usually, mail-out and web questionnaires do not require the researcher to seek consent *a priori*. Instead, consent is implied when the respondent completes and returns the survey. A sentence in the cover letter, on the survey instructions, or both that 'it is assumed that completion of this questionnaire indicates that consent to participate has been given' forewarns the respondent of the implied consent.

However, implied consent cannot always be assumed and you as a researcher must ensure that you are complying with ethics requirements. In the case of face-to-face or telephone interviews, it may be necessary to obtain formal informed consent by a signature on a consent form. Ethics requirements are specific to institutions and jurisdictions. As a researcher, you must consult the guidelines of the ethical review boards relevant to your research.

There is concern in the research community that emphasizing ethical issues of informed consent – including confidentiality, anonymity, the right to privacy, and minimal harm – may lead potential respondents to be suspicious of the research (Dillman, 2000; Grayson and Myles, 2004). However, the goal of ethical treatment of research participants outweighs arguments for reducing ethical rigour and reminds researchers of the need to conduct research that conforms to the tenet of minimal risk. Cover letters and consent forms can be artfully crafted to meet ethics requirements without turning off potential respondents.

The survey instrument

Chapter 5 provides a detailed account of developing survey items. Here, only the survey instructions are highlighted. It is usual to include completion instructions on the first page of a mail or web survey. These instructions should reinforce important elements contained in the cover letter without being repetitive. In addition, instructions specific to survey completion should be clear and easily readable. Figure 8.3 provides an example of the first page of a survey. The text in Figure 8.3 can be converted easily into a format to be used for telephone or face-to-face interviews.

Paths on Life's Way
Transitions of British Columbia Young Adults
in a Changing Society

Class of 2011, Life After High School!

Thank you for agreeing to participate in the *Class of 2011, Life After High School* questionnaire.

Your responses to the questions on this survey will provide vital information about the life transitions of your generation. Your participation will help us to continue to learn more about your educational, work, and other life experiences.

This questionnaire should take about 45 minutes to complete. Please read the instructions for each question carefully. If a written response is required, please ensure that your answer is easy to read.

This is a voluntary but important survey. All of the information that you provide in this questionnaire is strictly anonymous. Questionnaires contain identification numbers for statistical purposes only. All information that would permit identification of the individual will be removed.

You have the right to refuse to participate in this study. It is assumed that completion of this questionnaire indicates that consent to participate has been given.

Please complete all relevant sections.

Lesley Andres

Professor
Department of Educational Studies
University of British Columbia
tel: (604) 822-8943
fax: (604) 822-4244
email: lesley.andres@ubc.ca
web: http://www.edst.educ.ubc.ca/paths/paths.htm

Figure 8.3   Survey instructions

Incentives

Inclusion of an incentive in a survey package demonstrates an act of goodwill on the part of the researcher. When asking individuals to volunteer their time, the incentive serves as both a small gift and a way of thanking people for participating.

Research on incentives indicates that in the case of mail-out surveys, small financial incentives (between $2 and $5) that are sent with a survey package result in higher response rates than larger amounts ($10 or more) sent to only those who had completed the survey (Church, 1993). However, although the inclusion of cash in a survey package is strongly advocated by some, it may not be appropriate or desirable for all samples. For instance, $2 offered to some professional groups such as physicians may be considered insulting. In the case of web surveys, Bosnjak and Tuten (2003) demonstrated that neither a $2 incentive paid at the time of first contact, nor a promised incentive, affected the response rates of a sample of 1466 real estate brokers. However, the opportunity to be entered into a prize draw significantly increased both the response rate and the extent to which surveys were completed fully.

There are many other types of incentives to offer respondents. I have included refrigerator magnets in one of my survey mail-outs. The response rate for that study was 70%. In the 22-year follow-up of my longitudinal research project we included sticky notes printed with the study logo; the response rate to this phase was 79%. Other types of incentives that are not expensive and can be mailed easily are tote bags, USB sticks, or gift certificates for coffee.

TEXT BOX 8.2

Examples of incentives can be found on the following websites:

http://www.bicgraphic.ca/servlet/OnlineShopping/bgc?DSP=12&PCR=2:50000:50100:50110

http://ca.starline.com/catalog/view/Starline-Products/Bags/Totes/pg1

http://www.youngpro.com/products.htm

Providing incentives in a telephone survey may require that an initial contact letter be sent to the potential respondent. Along with the letter, an incentive can be included. For web surveys, potential respondents can be directed to a link that invites them, for example, to redeem coupons. In addition, links can be provided to reports or other websites that may be of interest to respondents.

Incentives are of interest to ethical review boards. Sometimes there is a fine line between incentive and coercion. An incentive turns into coercion when it results in 'undue inducement for participation, such as payments that would lead subjects to undertake actions that they would not normally accept' (http://rise.ubc.ca/helpCenter/GN/BREB_Guidance_Notes.html). In addition, offering prizes through lottery techniques must not violate gaming laws.

Following-up

Non-respondents to a survey may be systematically different from respondents. This topic is covered in detail in Chapter 7. In order to minimize the effects of non-response error, it is essential to enhance response rates by sending reminder postcards and second or even third copies of mail surveys or links to web surveys. The frequency and timing of reminders is addressed below.

Frequency

The usual reminder procedure for both mail and web surveys is as follows. First, after a period of time following the first survey a reminder postcard is sent. Those who do not respond are then sent a second survey. In the case of those who remain persistent non-responders, other forms of contact may be employed. With mail surveys, non-responders may be contacted by telephone or email. In this way, it is possible to confirm that their mailing information is correct. If incorrect, mailing addresses can be updated using conventional techniques such as electronic directories.

TEXT BOX 8.3

Online telephone directories

Australia	http://www.whitepages.com.au/
Canada	http://www.canada411.ca/
UK	http://www.192.com/
USA	http://www.whitepages.com/

In addition, we have used Facebook and LinkedIn to find respondents, with very good results. For web surveys, telephone contact serves a similar purpose. In other words, a different mode is used for follow-up. This signals to the respondent that their response is indeed important to the researcher.

In the case of telephone or face-to-face surveys, several attempts may be required to contact individuals. Persistence is essential to ensure that the ultimate sample is representative of the frame population.

Timing

Most survey texts prescribe time periods between follow-up contacts. In my experience, because every sample has its own unique qualities, it is more useful to monitor response rates and time the follow-ups accordingly. In Figure 8.4, questionnaire returns were plotted as they were received. When response rates began

---

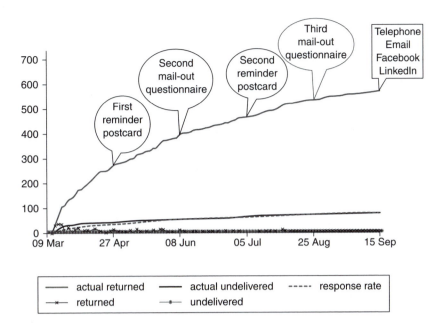

Figure 8.4 Survey follow-ups

to plateau, a reminder – either in the form of a reminder postcard or another survey package – was sent. Finally, follow-ups by telephone, email, or through social media sites such as Facebook and LinkedIn were conducted. The final response rate for this study was 79%.

Training interviewers

When surveys are administered by interviewers – either over the telephone or face-to-face – it is imperative that interviewers receive training in order to ensure that the goals of the study are accomplished. The role of the interviewer ranges from human automaton to engaged conversationalist. In the case of the former, the interviewer delivers the questionnaire exactly as it is scripted. When asked for clarification, the interviewer is trained only to repeat the question and nothing else. At the other end of the spectrum, the interviewer may ask a series of closed- and open-ended questions. S/he also uses the techniques of a skilled interviewer (Egan, 2010) which might include silence, repeating the question, and/or probing with the goal of inviting a more complete response.

The interviewer-administered survey delivery mode is extremely expensive in terms of time and money. When a strictly scripted approach to survey research is required, mail and web surveys are more cost-effective choices. This approach can be enriched by including a less rigid face-to-face or telephone interview component. Cresswell et al. (2008) offer several mixed methods designs that employ a more qualitative dimension such as interviews before, after, or concurrent with a more quantitative dimension such as self-administered surveys. Roulston (2010) provides an in-depth discussion of research interviewing.

In small-scale studies such as those undertaken in master's or doctoral research, it is ideal if the researcher conducts all of the interviews. S/he is able to bring the theoretical perspectives informing the study directly to the interview and can ensure consistency by approaching each interview in the same manner. Having conducted all the interviews will be a great asset when writing up the research in that the researcher will have first-hand experience of each interview. Also, conducting the interviews serves as an invaluable form of training for the fledgling researcher.

When it is not feasible for one person to conduct all of the interviewers, it will be necessary to employ and train interviewers. Interviewers must be apprised of the goals of the study and they must be well versed with the survey instrument and related questions. Also, they must be skilled at delivering the questions. The training process should include how the interviewers are to make initial contact with respondents. Coaching regarding voice intonation, non-verbal cues, pacing, and their role in providing clarification should be covered in the training sessions. Face-to-face interviewers require additional coaching regarding appropriate attire, and the effects of body language and facial expressions. If the survey contains open-ended questions, interviewers need to understand their role in eliciting appropriate responses.

In the delivery of face-to-face or telephone interviews, there is no 'one-size-fits-all' approach. The principal investigator and research team must decide on the extent to which the interview is scripted and train interviewers accordingly. Failure to do so may lead to an uneven approach to data collection due to interviewer effects. As a result, the trustworthiness of the findings may be compromised.

Summary

This chapter focused on the details of survey design and administration with the goal of enhancing response rates. Guidelines for the preparation of survey materials such as letters were offered. Ways to enhance the attractiveness of the survey instrument and related materials were provided. The use of appropriate incentives was encouraged. Finally, guidelines for following-up with respondents and the training of researchers were highlighted.

Exercises

1 Construct draft letters and consent forms as required for approval by your behavioural review ethics board.

2 Devise a detailed budget for your study. Provide detailed costs (e.g., printing, postage, data entry). Consider alternate scenarios and discuss the advantages and disadvantages of each.

3 Specify a schedule for your study, including timing of survey administration, plans for follow-up, and quality control.

4 Indicate the incentives that you will use in your study.

Further reading

Cresswell, J., Plano Clark, V. L., and Garrett, A. L. (2008). Methodological issues in conducting mixed methods research designs. In M. M. Bergman (ed.), *Advances in Mixed Methods Reserach* (pp. 66–83). London: Sage.
Ethics review documents from your institution or granting council.

NINE

Preparing for data analysis

It is not uncommon for students or researchers to collect data only to discover that they do not have access to required software, that they do not have any idea how to carry out analyses, or both. Anticipating how to conduct analyses must be part of the survey research design. In this chapter, I provide a description of how to produce 'code books' in advance of collecting data through the use of quantitative and qualitative software. Also, I describe how to anticipate transferring and entering data into various software packages. This discussion is linked with previous chapters on questionnaire design and survey formats and is intended to help readers avoid producing data that cannot be analysed or analysed to its full extent. Issues of data clean-up and coding of open-ended questions will also be addressed.

This chapter focuses on how to prepare your survey for analysis, *not* how to conduct analyses of survey data. Data analysis is a vast subject area that cannot be covered adequately in a few chapters of a survey methods book. Survey researchers need to acquire basic data analysis skills offered in introductory quantitative and qualitative methods courses. Once these basic skills are learned, and by completing additional advanced methods courses, you will have attained the skills to apply the most appropriate analytical method(s) to answer your research questions. A frequent mistake made by many researchers is to become an expert in a single method and then employ that method – regardless of the research question(s) – to analyse the data. As the saying goes, when given a hammer, everything starts to look like a nail. Such an approach to data analysis is often misguided and tends to give both quantitative and qualitative research bad reputations.

Cartoon 9.1

Although the specifics of data analysis are beyond the scope of this book, planning for data analysis is not. Before a survey is administered, you should have investigated which quantitative and qualitative data analysis software packages you will need. Cost will be a factor as these packages tend to be expensive. If your survey research project requires the manipulation of numbers, then you will need to purchase or have access to one or more statistical software programs. Manipulation of text gathered in open-ended questions on pen-and-paper or online surveys or through interviews conducted face-to-face, over the telephone, or via webcam can be conducted using either qualitative or quantitative software analysis programs. In Chapter 2, I described the various ways of obtaining the necessary software and related skill sets.

In this chapter, I use two software analysis programs – IBM SPSS (which stands for Statistical Package for the Social Sciences) and ATLAS.ti – to illustrate how to anticipate data analysis. Other software programs, such as SAS, Stata, NVivo, and MAXQDA, while having distinctive features, are in general similar to these two programs. Often, the choice of a program is guided by individual or specific institutional tastes. In order to gain first-hand experience while reading this chapter, a trial version of SPSS can be downloaded http://www14.software.ibm.com/download/data/web/en_US/trialprograms/W110742E06714B29.html. Also, within the SPSS program and elsewhere (e.g., http://pages.infinit.net/rlevesqu/spss.htm) more extensive tutorials are available.

Preparing a 'code book' in SPSS

Once your survey instrument has been developed, field tested or piloted, but before it has been administered, it is time to 'test-drive' it by preparing a 'code book'. Development of a code book allows you to specify the information about the variables in your survey. This information is both necessary for data analysis and provides detailed information about each variable. By working through the exercise of developing a code book before you have administered your survey, you will be able to detect any problems with your questions. Also, you can assess the labour intensiveness of data entry, which may result in a further revision of your survey instrument. Even if you are planning to administer a web survey where data entry is automatic, it is still a good idea to go through this exercise. As one of my statistics professors was fond of saying, you must 'marinate in your data'. This is the beginning phase of marinating.

In this section, I will use the spreadsheet in SPSS to illustrate how to develop a code book. The SPSS spreadsheet[3] offers two views: the data view (Figure 9.1) and

Figure 9.1 SPSS data view spreadsheet

Reprinted courtesy of International Business Machines Corporation, © SPSS, Inc., an IBM Company.

---

[3]Today's statistical software packages permit data entry through a spreadsheet. In addition, raw data can be imported from other formats such as Microsoft Excel or Access, and other statistical software packages such as SAS or Stata.

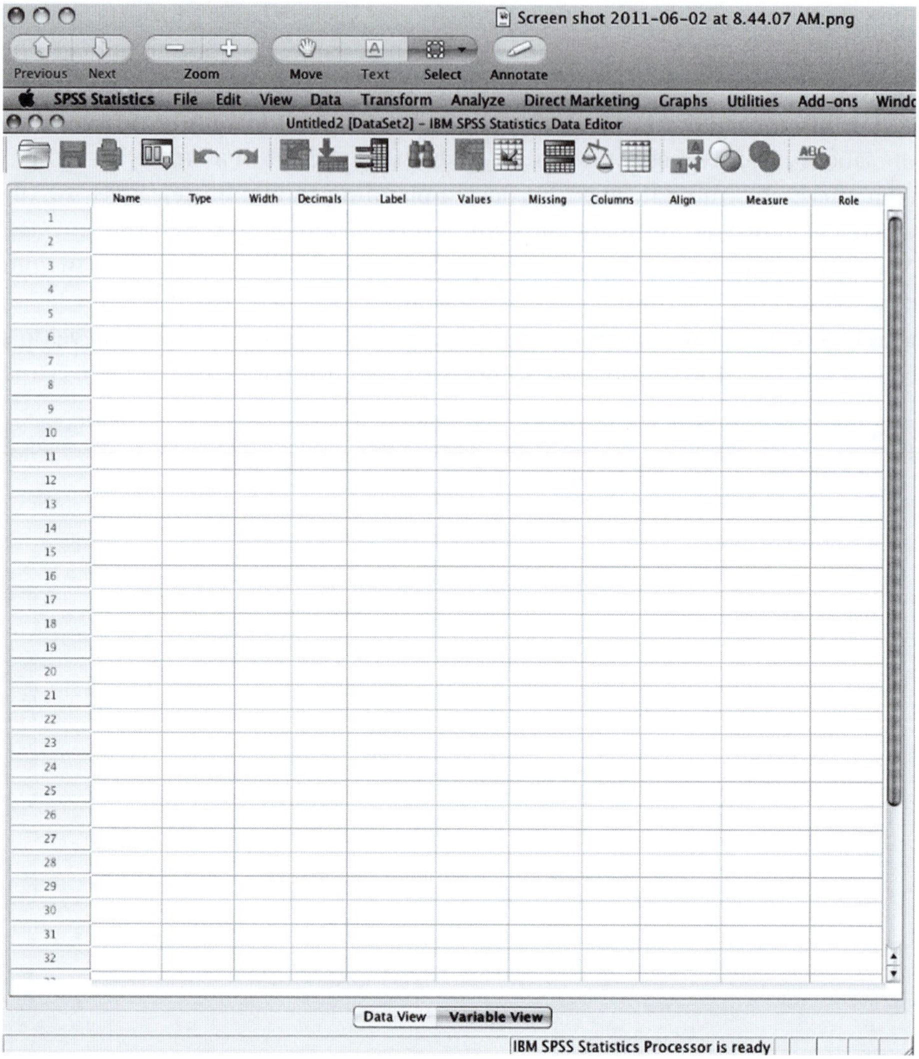

Figure 9.2 SPSS variable view spreadsheet

Reprinted courtesy of International Business Machines Corporation, © SPSS, Inc., an IBM Company.

the variable view (Figure 9.2). The variable view is used to specify the character-istics of each variable, and the data view is used to enter the data. To open the SPSS spreadsheet, select 'Type in Data' from the first screen that appears when the application is opened.

This survey in Example 9.1 exhibits many of the qualities of a good survey. It is attractive, the design is unique as it is printed on heavy paper, it is folded into the size of a double postcard, and it is illustrated. However, as we will see, the survey design can be improved.

Example 9.1   Example of a well-designed survey

Reprinted with the kind permission of Tinhorn Creek Vineyards
http://www.tinhorn.com/index.php.

This survey contains several variables. The parts of a variable include the following: variable name, type, variable width, decimal places, variable label, variable value, and missing specification. Other options for specifying variables are available in SPSS; however, the seven that are listed above are the most important for the beginning analyst. Each of these dimensions is described below.

Variable name

Each variable must be given a unique name. In SPSS, a variable name can contain 64 characters without spaces, with some limitations. For example, the character # cannot be used in a variable name. Other statistical programs limit the length of a variable name to eight characters; although it is not absolutely necessary, it might be good to get into the habit of doing so. Long variable names are also difficult to read. In the following examples, I try to keep the variable names rather short.

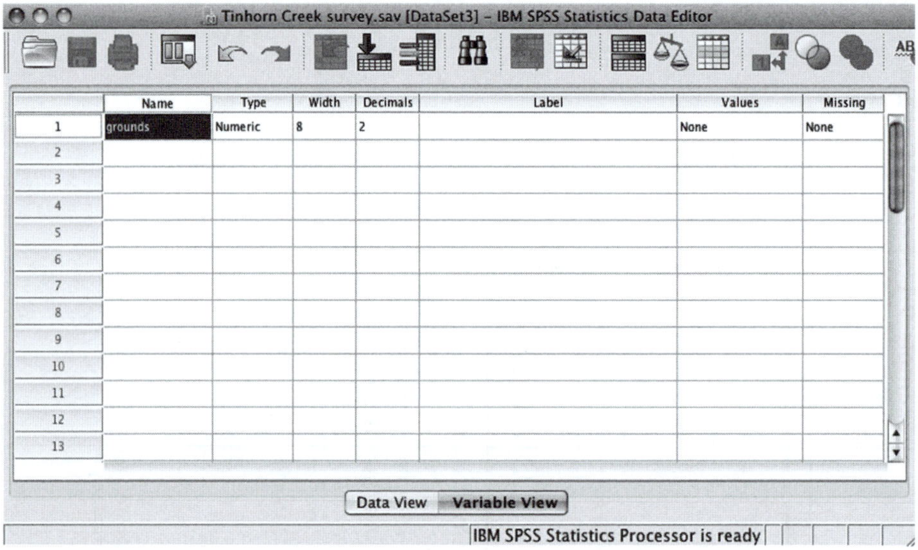

	Name	Type	Width	Decimals	Label	Values	Missing
1	grounds	Numeric	8	2		None	None
2							
3							
4							
5							
6							
7							
8							
9							
10							
11							
12							
13							

Data View   **Variable View**

IBM SPSS Statistics Processor is ready

Figure 9.3   Variable name

Reprinted courtesy of International Business Machines Corporation, © SPSS, Inc., an IBM Company.

The first component in the survey is under the topic 'Presentation and Appearance'. However, this heading is not a variable because there will be no data associated with it. The variables are 'grounds', 'facilities,' and 'overall cleanliness.' To begin, in Figure 9.3, I give the first variable the name 'grounds'.

Variable type

As portrayed in Figure 9.4, many different types of variables can be specified. The most common types of variables are 'numeric' and 'string'. With numeric variables, only numbers (e.g., 134, 23, 6) can be entered as a value. String variables may contain letters and numbers (e.g., Canadian or UK postal codes), or letters only. Whenever possible, numeric variables should be used because analyses employing string variables have many limitations. For example, if your survey asks respondents to identify if they are female or male, one way to enter this information is to use the string 'female' or 'male'. However, it is much better to convert the letters into numeric variables 1=female and 0=male. Variable values will be explained more fully below.

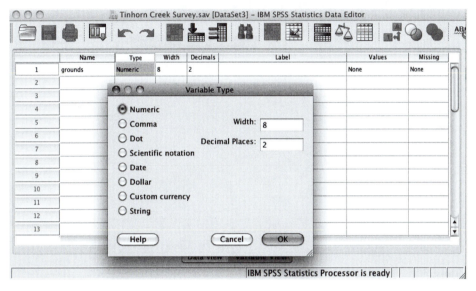

Figure 9.4   Variable type

Reprinted courtesy of International Business Machines Corporation, © SPSS, Inc., an IBM Company.

Variable width

By default, the variable width is specified as '8' (see Figure 9.4). This means that the variable displayed in the Data Editor will be allowed a column width of '8' including decimal places. The variable width can be adjusted as necessary, but usually the default value is adequate.

Decimals

By default, variables are assigned two decimal places (Figure 9.4). If there is no need for one or more decimal places, change this value to '0' as the data output will be easier to read.

Variable labels

The variable name, if kept short, does not provide very much information about the variable. In the value label column, much more description – up to 256 characters – of the variable can be included. It is a good practice to include the entire stem of the question in the value label column. In Figure 9.5, I have given the variable a question number 'Q1a' and the description 'Presentation and Appearance: Grounds'. More information can be provided so that you can remind yourself of the features of this variable.

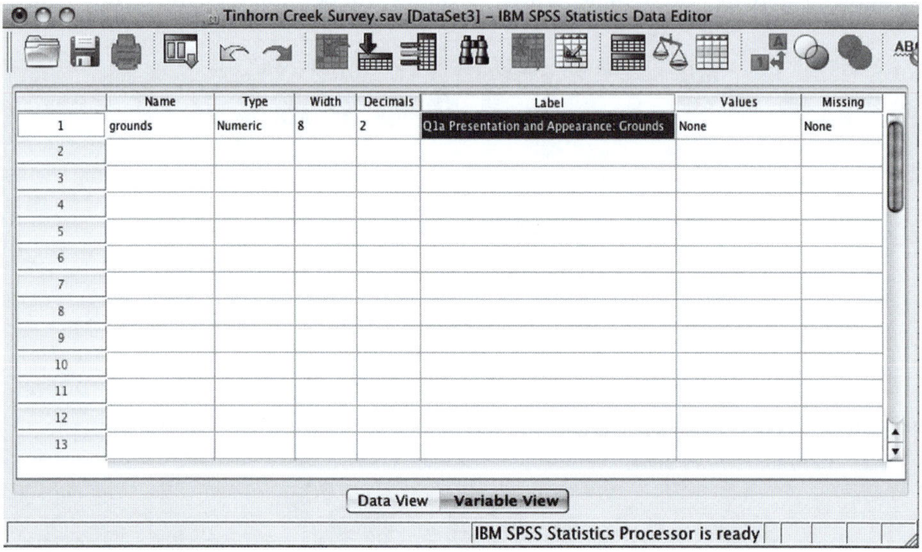

Figure 9.5   Variable labels

Reprinted courtesy of International Business Machines Corporation, © SPSS, Inc., an IBM Company.

Values and their related labels

Values and their labels identify the data contained in the spreadsheet data view (Figure 9.6). Some variables do not need any identification. For example, if you have asked respondents to identify their birth year, the information provided would be entered into the data view spreadsheet (e.g., 1980, 1972). In the variable view, the value label would remain 'none' which is the default variable.

When data are categorical – that is, when numbers are employed to represent categories – the actual numerical values and their related labels need to be identified. For the 'grounds' variable, respondents are asked to respond by identifying a value on a five-point scale. The scale ranges from 'needs improvement' to 'best'.

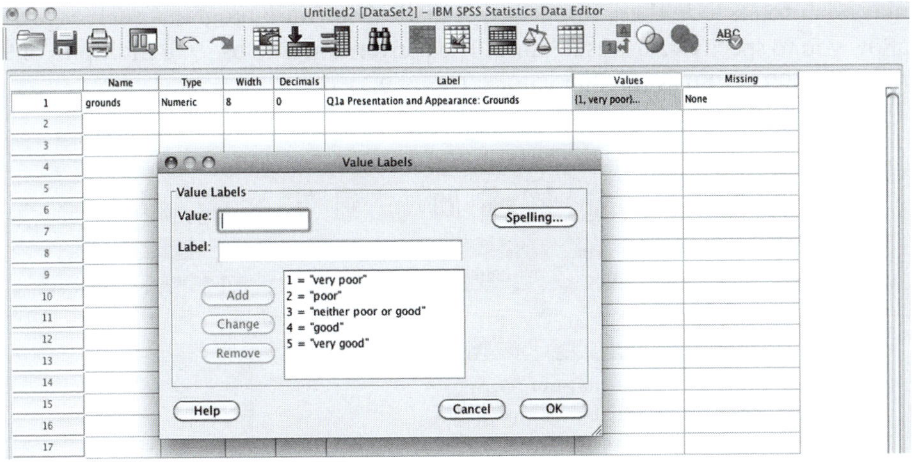

Figure 9.6 Values and their Related Labels

Reprinted courtesy of International Business Machines Corporation, © SPSS, Inc., an IBM Company.

Now we encounter a problem with the questionnaire. A five-point scale implies a continuum from least to most. However, each point in the scale does not have a distinctive label. The values are 1, 2, 3, 4, and 5. But what labels should we assign to these values? While the value '5' seems clearly associated with the label 'best', the values 1, 2, and 3 seem to be related to 'needs improvement'. The label for the value '4' is not at all clear. If we are not clear about the value labels, it is likely that respondents were not clear about what was being requested of them. Working through the identification of a code book in this penultimate stage of survey design provides you with the opportunity to tweak the questionnaire so that all questions and their related scales are clear. The existing scale for this question can be revised as follows: 1 = very poor, 2 = poor, 3 = neither poor nor good, 4 = good, 5 = very good. The new scale is balanced and each point on the scale has its own unique label (Figure 9.6). The survey instrument now needs to be revised to include the new scale. Value labels are entered in the column 'Label'.

Missing values

Missing values take two forms: those that are *system missing*, and those that are *identified missing*. System missing variables are simply data cells without any values, indicating that for a variety of reasons the respondent has not answered the question. Sometimes, even when the respondent has answered the question, it may be analytically useful to declare the value missing. For example, respondents may answer the 'not applicable' option on a scale. For some analyses, you may wish to exclude these responses. Statistical software programs such as SPSS allow you to specify values as missing. The convention is to use 9 or multiples of 9 (e.g., 99, 999, 9999) as missing values (Figure 9.7).

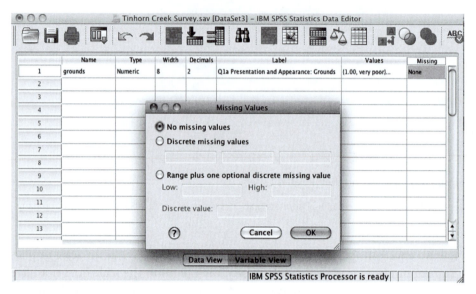

Figure 9.7 Missing values

Reprinted courtesy of International Business Machines Corporation, © SPSS, Inc., an IBM Company.

Because the values used to specify variable 'grounds' range from 1 to 5, missing values can be identified as '9'. To enter user-defined missing values, click on 'Discrete missing values' and enter the values you have chosen.

The variables 'grounds' through to 'rating of the overall experience' share the same structure. To create identifying information for these variables, the steps above are replicated. In Figure 9.8, all of the information for these variables has been identified.

Open-ended questions

The next three questions 'What did you like best about us?', 'What could we improve?' and 'What events would you like us to hold?' do not provide respondents with pre-identified responses. Instead, respondents are invited to write in answers. Because we do not know the responses in advance, only variable names can be entered (Figure 9.9); the values and related labels column cannot be identified at this point. Open-ended questions are discussed more fully later in this chapter.

Figure 9.8 Specification of the first part of the survey

Reprinted courtesy of International Business Machines Corporation, © SPSS, Inc., an IBM Company.

	Name	Type	Width	Decimals	Label	Values	Missing
1	grounds	Numeric	8	0	Q1a Presentation and Appearance: Grounds	{1, very poor}...	None
2	facilities	Numeric	8	0	Q1b Presentation and Appearance: Facilities	{1, very poor}...	None
3	cleanliness	Numeric	8	0	Q1c Presentation and Appearance: Overall Cleanliness	{1, very poor}...	None
4	staffknowledge	Numeric	8	0	Q2a Quality of Experience: Knowledge of Staff	{1, very poor}...	None
5	friendliness	Numeric	8	0	Q2b Quality of Experience: Friendliness	{1, very poor}...	None
6	helpfulness	Numeric	8	0	Q2c Quality of Experience: Helpfulness	{1, very poor}...	None
7	winequal	Numeric	8	0	Q3a Products: Quality of Wines	{1, very poor}...	None
8	nonwinemerch	Numeric	8	0	Q3b Products: Non-wine Merchandise	{1, very poor}...	None
9	overallrating	Numeric	8	0	Q4 Rating of Overall Experience	{1, very poor}...	None
10	likebest1	Numeric	8	0	Q5 What did you like best about us?	None	None
11	improve	Numeric	8	0	Q6 What could we improve?	None	None
12	events	Numeric	8	0	Q7 What events would you like us to hold?	None	None
13							
14							

Figure 9.9 Open-ended questions

Reprinted courtesy of International Business Machines Corporation, © SPSS, Inc., an IBM Company.

Multiple response items

The next question, 'How did you hear about us?', invites the respondent to identify the sources of information that informed visitors to Tinhorn Creek Vineyards. Eight different sources and one 'other' category are specified. This question contains two survey design flaws. First, the question does not contain any instructions to guide respondents. Should respondents identify all of the sources of information that they used or only the most important source of information? One could guess that respondents are being invited to provide the former; however, it is not clear. To ensure that each respondent interprets the question in the same way, the instruction 'Check all that apply' needs to be added.

In addition, several of the items are double-barrelled. The 'newspaper/*Wine Trails*' variable collapses these items 'newspaper' and the specific *Wine Trails* newspaper into one category. Perhaps the distinction between the two variables is not important. However, if the winery had paid for extensive advertising in *Wine Trails*, it may be of great interest to be able to determine how many visitors identified this specific newspaper as a source of information. It is always best to avoid double-barrelled responses. Remember that data can always be aggregated up, but never disaggregated down.

To enter the data for these questions, the steps above could be followed and values could be 0=no and 1=yes for each item. However, there is a more efficient and versatile way of setting up these types of variables. Instead of dichotomous yes/no values for each variable, the *multiple responses* variable type is used. A multiple

	Name	Type	Width	Decimals	Label	Values	Missing
1	grounds	Numeric	8	0	Q1a Presentation and Appearance: Grounds	{1, very poor}...	None
2	facilities	Numeric	8	0	Q1b Presentation and Appearance: Facilities	{1, very poor}...	None
3	cleanliness	Numeric	8	0	Q1c Presentation and Appearance: Overall Cleanliness	{1, very poor}...	None
4	staffknowledge	Numeric	8	0	Q2a Quality of Experience: Knowledge of Staff	{1, very poor}...	None
5	friendliness	Numeric	8	0	Q2b Quality of Experience: Friendliness	{1, very poor}...	None
6	helpfulness	Numeric	8	0	Q2c Quality of Experience: Helpfulness	{1, very poor}...	None
7	winequal	Numeric	8	0	Q3a Products: Quality of Wines	{1, very poor}...	None
8	nonwinemerch	Numeric	8	0	Q3b Products: Non-wine Merchandise	{1, very poor}...	None
9	overallrating	Numeric	8	0	Q4 Rating of Overall Experience	{1, very poor}...	None
10	likebest1	Numeric	8	0	Q5 What did you like best about us?	None	None
11	improve	Numeric	8	0	Q6 What could we improve?	None	None
12	events	Numeric	8	0	Q7 What events would you like us to hold?	None	None
13	hearabout1	Numeric	8	0	Q8a How did you hear about us?	{1, newspaper}...	None
14	hearabout2	Numeric	8	0	Q8b How did you hear about us?	{1, newspaper}...	None
15	hearabout3	Numeric	8	0	Q8c How did you hear about us?	{1, newspaper}...	None
16	hearabout4	Numeric	8	0	Q8d How did you hear about us?	{1, newspaper}...	None
17	hearaobut5	Numeric	9	0	Q8e How did you hear about us?	{1, newspaper}...	None
18							
19							
20							

Figure 9.10 Multiple response sets

Reprinted courtesy of International Business Machines Corporation, © SPSS, Inc., an IBM Company.

response approach allows a group of variables such as these to be analysed as a set. Instead of following the procedures employed above, variables to be used in a set are defined as follows. Each variable in the set is provided with a unique but similar name. In the example, I have used the names 'hearabout1' through to 'hearabout5' (Figure 9.10). Although there are eight possible choices (newspaper to radio/TV), it is highly unlikely that a single respondent will have used all eight sources. An educated guess of the likely number of responses by any one respondent is made. I have guessed that the maximum number of responses by one respondent will be five. If this guess turns out to be inaccurate, additional variables can be added as necessary.

With multiple response sets, the values and related labels are of a different nature than have been described in the previous examples. Rather than specifying value labels for a single variable, the same value labels are provided for the entire set of a variables. In Figure 9.11, each item specified is listed, not as a variable, but as a value label.

Data corresponding to the value labels for this multiple response question will be entered into the data view spreadsheet. For example, if respondent 1 indicated that she had heard about the winery from the newspaper and wine store, the value '1' would be entered into the cell for the 'hearabout1' variable and '5'

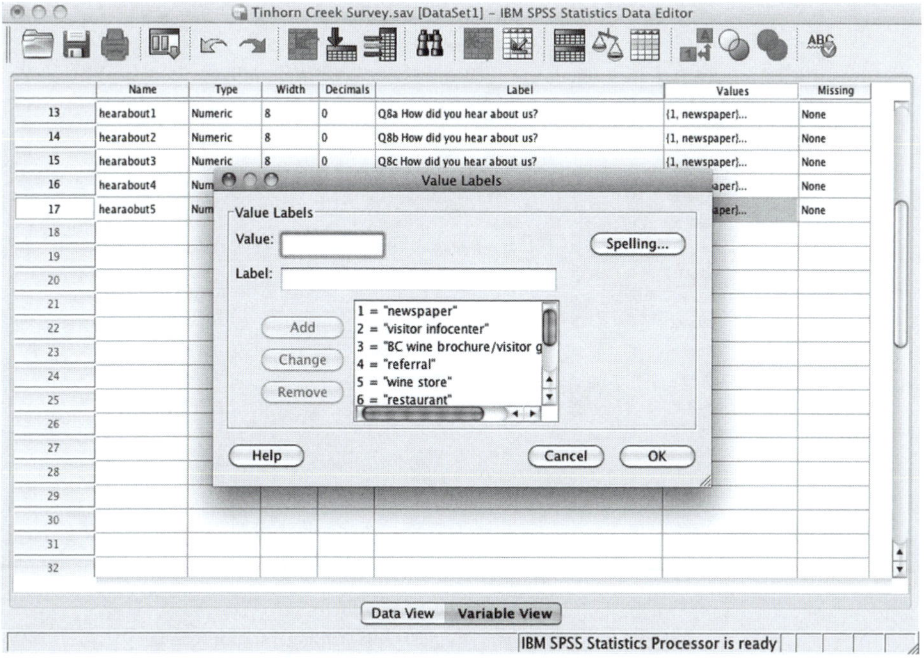

Figure 9.11   Values and their related labels for multiple response sets

Reprinted courtesy of International Business Machines Corporation, © SPSS, Inc., an IBM Company.

for the 'hearabout2' variable. If respondent 2 checked newspaper, restaurant, and hotel/motel, the value '1' would be entered into the cell for the 'hearabout1' variable and 6 for the 'hearabout2' variable, and 7 for 'hearabout3'. To analyse the data, the command 'Multiple Response' and subcommand 'Define Multiple Response Sets' under the 'Analyze' tab in SPSS is used to create the multiple response variable. The subcommands 'Frequencies' and 'Crosstabulations' under the command 'Multiple Response' are used to analyse multiple response variables.

Also, the question 'How did you hear about us?' contains three open-ended questions. In order to analyse these questions in SPSS, separate variables must be created (lines 18–20 in Figure 9.12). Also, the 'Other – please specify' option can be set up as an open-ended question.

The question 'Would you like to receive our quarterly newsletter?' can be identified in the same manner as for 'grounds' above. The values and related labels can be specified as 1=yes, 0=no.

	Name	Type	Width	Decimals	Label	Values	Missing
1	ID	Numeric	8	0	respondent identification number	None	None
2	grounds	Numeric	8	0	Q1a Presentation and Appearance: Grounds	{1, very poor}...	None
3	facilities	Numeric	8	0	Q1b Presentation and Appearance: Facilities	{1, very poor}...	None
4	cleanliness	Numeric	8	0	Q1c Presentation and Appearance: Overall Cleanliness	{1, very poor}...	None
5	staffknowledge	Numeric	8	0	Q2a Quality of Experience: Knowledge of Staff	{1, very poor}...	None
6	friendliness	Numeric	8	0	Q2b Quality of Experience: Friendliness	{1, very poor}...	None
7	helpfulness	Numeric	8	0	Q2c Quality of Experience: Helpfulness	{1, very poor}...	None
8	winequal	Numeric	8	0	Q3a Products: Quality of Wines	{1, very poor}...	None
9	nonwinemerch	Numeric	8	0	Q3b Products: Non-wine Merchandise	{1, very poor}...	None
10	overallrating	Numeric	8	0	Q4 Rating of Overall Experience	{1, very poor}...	None
11	likebest1	Numeric	8	0	Q5 What did you like best about us?	None	None
12	improve	Numeric	8	0	Q6 What could we improve?	None	None
13	events	Numeric	8	0	Q7 What events would you like us to hold?	None	None
14	hearabout1	Numeric	8	0	Q8a How did you hear about us?	{1, newspaper}...	None
15	hearabout2	Numeric	8	0	Q8b How did you hear about us?	{1, newspaper}...	None
16	hearabout3	Numeric	8	0	Q8c How did you hear about us?	{1, newspaper}...	None
17	hearabout4	Numeric	8	0	Q8d How did you hear about us?	{1, newspaper}...	None
18	hearaobut5	Numeric	9	0	Q8e How did you hear about us?	{1, newspaper}...	None
19	referralname	Numeric	8	0	Q9 Referral name	None	None
20	winestorename	Numeric	8	0	Q10 Wine store name	None	None
21	restaurantname	Numeric	8	0	Q11 Restaurant name	None	None
22	newsletter	Numeric	8	0	Q12 Would you like to receive our quarterly newsletter?	{0, no}...	None
23							

Data View **Variable View**

IBM SPSS Statistics Processor is ready

Figure 9.12 Code book for the entire survey

Reprinted courtesy of International Business Machines Corporation, © SPSS, Inc., an IBM Company.

Finally, in the last segment of the survey, respondent identification information is requested. From an ethics perspective, this information should be stored separately from the information collected on the survey. However, a link between the survey responses and the respondent can be made by assigning a unique identification number to each survey. This number is also recorded in the database containing the names and addresses of respondents. The identification number (ID) is logically the first variable contained in the data file.

In Figure 9.12, all of the variables in this survey have been identified. Survey design errors have been corrected, and after having revised the survey accordingly, it is ready for administration. As responses are received, the data can be entered into the spreadsheet.

Even in a short questionnaire such as the Tinhorn Creek Vineyards survey, several different types of question format have been used. These include closed-ended dichotomous and Likert-type questions, questions that can be analysed through a multiple response approach, and open-ended questions. In addition, a separate database of names and addresses of visitors to the winery will have been generated. This exercise also highlights the data analysis skill sets that you will need to analyse your survey data.

A more detailed look at open-ended questions

In the example above, the open-ended questions are designed to generate short answers. Also, because of the nature of the questions, the range of responses will be limited. In terms of analysis, the responses can simply be provided with a discrete code and a list of responses can be generated.

Such a straightforward approach is not always possible with responses to open-ended questions. In the following pages, by employing examples, I provide a few different approaches to the analysis of responses to open-ended questions.

Be careful what you ask

A few years ago, I volunteered to assist the student representative of the Canadian Society for the Study of Higher Education (CSSHE) to analyse the findings of a survey that they had administered to the student members. I was teaching a graduate-level course entitled 'Analyzing Survey Data' and I thought that this short four-page survey with 26 responses would serve as a good way to introduce my class to data entry.

How wrong I was! It turned out that the entire survey was comprised of open-ended questions. Data entry and analysis was extremely time-consuming. In the end, however, the resulting report provided a very rich and detailed account of

Figure 9.13   CSSHE student survey

Reprinted with the kind permission of the Canadian Society for the Study of Higher Education.

the student members of the CSSHE. Figure 9.13 shows the first question of this survey. This question generated 80 unique responses, representing on average three responses per respondent.

In Table 9.1, the 80 responses have been categorized under 14 themes. Generation of these themes was carried out inductively. That is, the graduate students enrolled in this course first generated the entire list of responses; then, based on their knowledge of the field and subfields, they generated themes and subsumed the descriptors under these themes. Of course, the themes are subjective; another class of students could have generated a somewhat different set of themes. Judgement calls play a role in all research.

In subsequent research, the 14 themes generated by the open-ended question on the CSSHE survey could be used to construct a closed-ended question as in Example 9.2.

Table 9.1   Categories of descriptors of students' theses or projects

1	**Gender Studies** equity feminist pedagogy gender discrimination gender equity women women faculty women studies	**6**	**Faculty Development** benchmarks continuing professional education disciplinary culture evaluation of teaching faculty faculty development professional collaboration teaching knowledge	**11**	**Professions** health professions nutrition police professions scope of practice unions
2	**Critical Theory** critical feminism critical pedagogy critical theory power			**12**	**Language &** **Nationalism** Atlantic Canada language nationalism

		7	**Technology**
			innovation
			online learning
			   communities
			technology
				13	**Theory & Policy**
					activity theory
					collaborative action
					   research
					education policy
					philosophy of body
					policy
					qualitative
					queer theory
					social theory

3	**College Vocational**
	college
	community colleges
	employability skills
	development
	school–work
	   transitions
	vocational and
	   applied education
		8	**Teaching & Learning**
			curriculum
			instructional psychology
			knowledge construction
			knowledge production
			knowledge transfer
			physics education
			problem-based learning
			reflective practice		

4	**Indigenous Studies**
	aboriginal post-
	   secondary students
	indigenous
	   methodology
	indigenous student
	   success
		9	**Colonialism**
			anti-racism
			decolonization methods
			post-colonial studies
			race
			racial equity
			violence
				14	**Other**
					Biglan
					academic disciplines
					commercialization
					international
					   education

5	**Higher Education**
	academic culture
	administration
	   education
	educational leadership
	educational theory
	higher education
	higher education
	   administration
	university rankings
	university industry links
		10	**Students**
			academic advising
			graduate education
			plagiarism
			pre-service
			admission policy
			retention/persistence
			student decision-making
			student services		

Reprinted with the kind permission of the Canadian Society for the Study of Higher Education.

Example 9.2   Converting an open-ended question into a closed-ended question

Which of the following descriptors best describe the research areas associated with your thesis or project? (Check one for each line)

		Yes	No
a.	College vocational	$\square_1$	$\square_0$
b.	Colonialism	$\square_1$	$\square_0$
c.	Critical theory	$\square_1$	$\square_0$
d.	Faculty development	$\square_1$	$\square_0$
e.	Gender studies	$\square_1$	$\square_0$
f.	Higher education	$\square_1$	$\square_0$
g.	Indigenous studies	$\square_1$	$\square_0$
h.	Language & nationalism	$\square_1$	$\square_0$
i.	Professions	$\square_1$	$\square_0$
j.	Students	$\square_1$	$\square_0$
k.	Teaching and learning	$\square_1$	$\square_0$
l.	Technology	$\square_1$	$\square_0$
m.	Theory and policy	$\square_1$	$\square_0$
n.	Other (specify) _____	$\square_1$	$\square_0$
o.	Other (specify) _____	$\square_1$	$\square_0$
p.	Other (specify) _____	$\square_1$	$\square_0$

Entering more extensive open-ended responses into SPSS

When open-ended questions are part of a large survey which also contains responses to closed-ended questions, it is ideal to also enter the responses to the open-ended questions into the statistical software program. In doing so, open-ended questions can be analysed in relation to the other variables. For example, I asked the question in Example 9.3 in the 22-year follow-up of my Paths on Life's Way longitudinal study. Over 90% of respondents completed both the closed-ended Likert-type questions and the open-ended questions (Andres, 2010).

Example 9.3   A combined closed- and open-ended question

45.a. To what extent has the economic recession that began in 2008 affected you and your family? (Check **one for each line**)

	Extent of Effect:				
	Strong Negative Effect	Negative Effect	Positive Effect	Strong Positive Effect	Not Applicable
a. My work or career	$\square_1$	$\square_2$	$\square_3$	$\square_4$	$\square_5$
b. My personal life	$\square_1$	$\square_2$	$\square_3$	$\square_4$	$\square_5$
c. My ability to provide the essentials for my family	$\square_1$	$\square_2$	$\square_3$	$\square_4$	$\square_5$
d. My ability to provide 'extras' for my family	$\square_1$	$\square_2$	$\square_3$	$\square_4$	$\square_5$
e. My personal savings	$\square_1$	$\square_2$	$\square_3$	$\square_4$	$\square_5$
f. My retirement savings (e.g., RRSPs)	$\square_1$	$\square_2$	$\square_3$	$\square_4$	$\square_5$
g. My children's education savings (e.g., RESPs)	$\square_1$	$\square_2$	$\square_3$	$\square_4$	$\square_5$

45.b. Please explain your answers to **Question 45.a.**

_____

_____

_____

_____

The open-ended component of this question (45.b) resulted in 44 pages of text. Because both the quantitative and qualitative data are contained in the same data analysis program, I am able to analyse the open-ended responses by gender, post-secondary completion status, socio-economic status, or any other of the thousands of variables in this data set. Using moderating variables such as gender, the text can be extracted separately for women and men. It can be quantified by counting instances of certain types of statements and generating themes in the same manner as was done in Table 9.1. In addition, the more extensive comments can be used to enrich our understandings of the phenomena under investigation.

In Example 9.4, I provide an example of some of the analyses generated from responses to the open-ended questions. The sample is split by educational homogamy group and gender. The variable 'educational homogamy' was constructed by determining who married whom. The definition of a low-homogamy couple was one in which neither person had earned a university degree. High-homogamy couples were comprised of both persons with university degrees. In addition, the two groups were further divided by gender. I extracted the text by homogamy group and gender using SPSS, then I quantified the responses into the categories presented in Example 9.4. Then I returned to the text to explain the percentages, as shown in Example 9.5.

Example 9.4   Quantification of responses to an open-ended question

	Females		Males	
	Low	High	Low	High
No effect	39	56	28	43
Job negative	28	16	17	8
Job positive	3	5	7	10
Two incomes	14	15	2	5
Savings ↓	21	21	22	41
Savings ↑	21	9	2	14
Feeling pinch	15	11	11	4

Example 9.5 demonstrates that 28% of low-homogamy women and 16% of high-homogamy women wrote responses in the open-ended question that the 2008 financial crisis had had a negative effect on their job. However, by further scrutinizing the comments, the negative effect was different for each group of women. However, of the high-homogamy women, 54% described the negative effect as a change in work conditions or a cut in salary and benefits,

and 46% described the negative effect as job loss. The comparative proportions for low-homogamy women were 36% and 64%, respectively. The example illustrates that while data reduction in terms of themes can be efficient, important information can be lost.

Example 9.5 Employing open-ended comments to explain the frequencies of responses

	Females		Males	
	Low	High	Low	High
No effect	39	56	28	43
Job negative	28	16		8

Negative Effect 36%

I had to take a 6% wage decrease since last May + my husband's business he started in 2007 has been affected as well.

Our office has downsized, additional stress/ pressure, less hours not when wanted.

Job Loss 64%

Have been on and off E.I. Currently on EI waiting for economy to turn around. Relationship of 21 years split up.

My husband was laid off in 2008 & with this our main income disappeared.

Feeling p.   11

Negative Effect 54%

Had decrease in yearly salary/benefits/etc.

I still receive the same amount of pay as a teacher, but there were cuts to education . . . . My husband's work was more severely affected which meant cutting back on the "extras," as well as less savings.

Job Loss 46%

My husband experience 3 months of reduced/no work.

My husband has lost his job 2x in past 3 years.

Not my work - my husband's.

Qualitative purists resist counting because they argue that it violates the goal of mining the data for meanings and understandings. However, by counting instances, the researcher is able to assess the extent to which such comments exist in the data. Assessing the magnitude of responses gives an account of the 'oomph' factor, described by Ziliak and McCloskey (2008) as 'how much and who cares?'. Morever, it prevents the tendency to *code for* [and emphasize] the exotic, the bizarre, the violent' (Fine et al., 2000: 118). By using a mixed methods approach to data analysis – that is, employing 'multiple ways to make sense of the world' (Greene, 2007: 20), it is possible to portray a much more rich and accurate account.

Analysing qualitative data with qualitative software

For survey research projects containing only transcript data collected through inter-views, it may be preferable to use a qualitative software package to analyse the data. There are many qualitative software packages from which to choose. ATLAS.ti is one package and in this section I provide an overview of how it can be used to analyse open-ended responses collected through one or more data collection modes. It is beyond the scope of this section to present the many features of ATLAS.ti, which go beyond analyses of text. The purpose of this section is to provide a brief introduction to the program. Severa l resources can be used in conjunction with this introduction – for example, the ATLAS.ti website (http://www.atlasti.com/) and related documents such as Quick Tour (http://www.atlasti.com/quicktour.html), along with Muhr and Friese (2004). Also, 'survey import' is a new feature in ATLAS.ti 6. Through this feature, results of online surveys can be converted automatically into projects called 'hermeneutic units' in ATLAS.ti. Details are available at http://www.atlasti.com/surveys0.html.

The first step in data preparation is to transcribe the text using any word-processing program and save it in rich text format.[4] One or more documents can be prepared. Next, the documents must be read into the ATLAS.ti. Before doing so, a project or 'hermeneutic unit' (HU) must be created (Figures 9.14a and 9.14b) in ATLAS.ti. Click on 'File,' and then 'New Hermenueutic Unit.' The HU is assigned a name and saved.

Once the HU has been created, one or more documents can be read into the pro-gram. In the example in Figure 9.15, documents are read into one hermeneutic unit (HU).

Coding is carried out on one document at a time. In Figure 9.16, one of the ten documents assigned to the HU titled 'homogamy 2010' is open and available for coding.

Once the documents have been read in, coding can commence. In qualitative software packages, codes are the equivalent of variables. The conceptual frame-work developed earlier in your survey project can serve as a starting point to generate one or more codes. The codes may be the names of your constructs, such as 'subjective well-being' or 'happiness'. However, unlike variable specification for closed-ended questions as described at the beginning of this chapter, for the most part codes for open-ended questions cannot be generated *a priori*. Rather, codes are usually developed inductively through the analysis of the text. In other words, the text speaks to the researcher, who, in turn, generates codes from the text.

Coding can take several forms. For the beginner, free coding is a good place to start. First, you must select the text for which you wish to apply the new code. Next, under the 'Codes' tab, select 'Create Free Code' (see Figures 9.17a and 9.17b).

---

[4]Other formats such as plain text, Word documents, and HTML can be used. However, because ATLAS.ti is designed for rich text, it is used in this example.

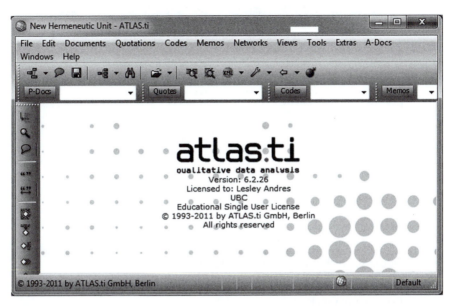

Figure 9.14a Creating a hermeneutic unit (HU), step one

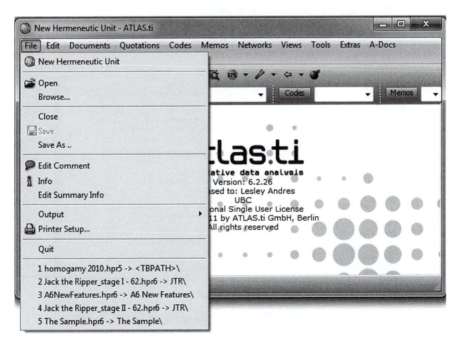

Figure 9.14b Creating a hermeneutic unit (HU), step two

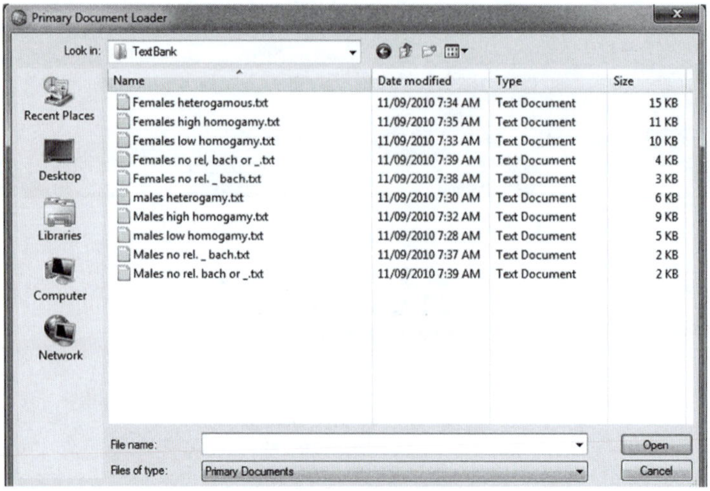

Figure 9.15 Reading in primary documents

Reprinted with the kind permission of ATLAS.ti Scientific Software Development GmbH.

Figure 9.16 Opening documents in ATLAS.ti

Reprinted with the kind permission of ATLAS.ti Scientific Software Development GmbH.

Codes such as 'no overall effect' can be entered (Figure 9.18). Once the code is created, it is listed in the coding menu and can be reused to code corresponding text with a given code. Also, the code appears in the margin area (the right-hand side of the screen).

The remaining text can be coded by using a combination of free coding and coding from the list in the Codes menu. In Figure 9.19, at the right-hand side of the screenshot, multiple codes generated in ATLAS.ti are visible.

Codes and their related quotations can be generated using the 'query tool' (the binoculars in the second menu bar). It is possible to create a list of quotations by using each code or two or more codes, for example 'no overall effect' and 'no effect on job,' as portrayed in Figure 9.20.

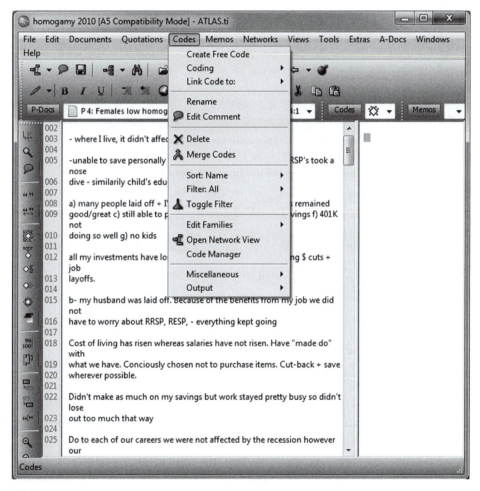

Figure 9.17a Creating a free code, step one

Reprinted with the kind permission of ATLAS.ti Scientific Software Development GmbH.

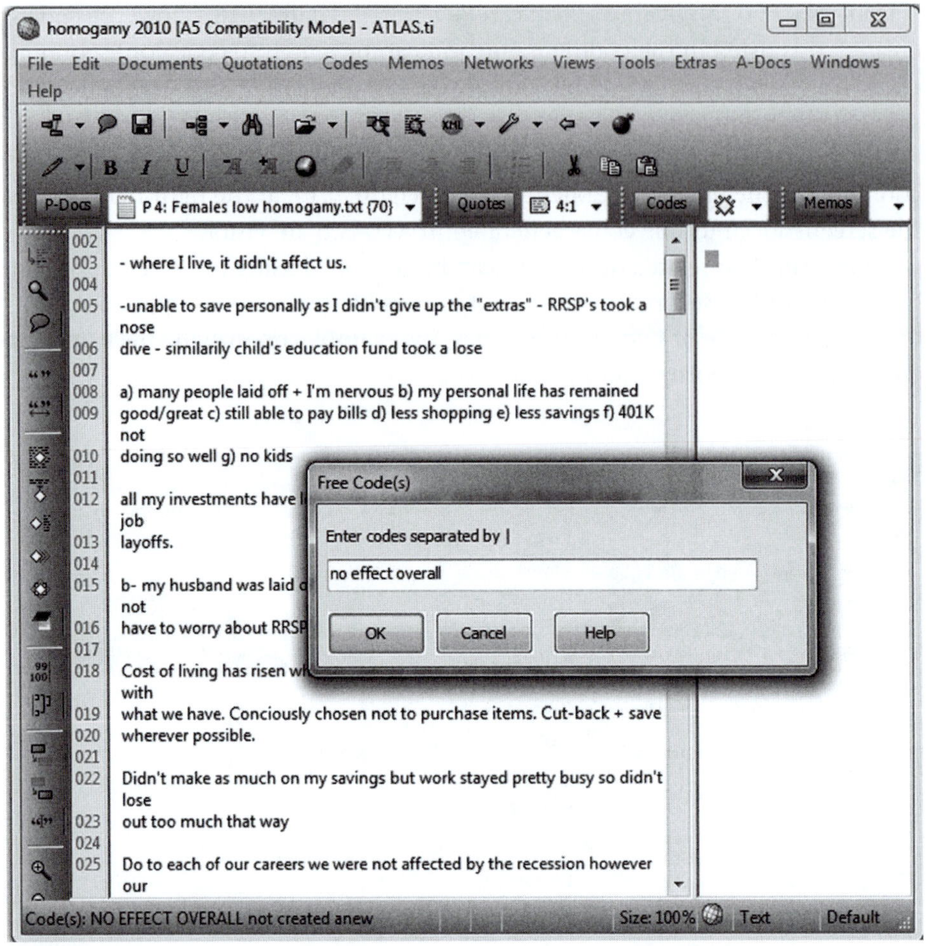

Figure 9.17b Creating a free code, step two

Reprinted with the kind permission of ATLAS.ti Scientific Software Development GmbH.

SPSS export function in ATLAS.ti

It may be desirable to analyse the text generated from interview data further by quantifying it. In ATLAS.ti it is possible to convert codes into variables and generate SPSS syntax containing variable definitions (variable names and labels, and values and labels) and the related data matrix. The data can be imported into SPSS and analysed. The SPSS export command can be found in the 'Extras' tab in the menu bar (Figure 9.21). When this feature is selected, SPSS syntax and the data matrix are generated (Figure 9.22), both of which can be read into SPSS. Data that began as text can now be analysed quantitatively in SPSS.

Figure 9.18   Coding text

Reprinted with the kind permission of ATLAS.ti Scientific Software Development GmbH.

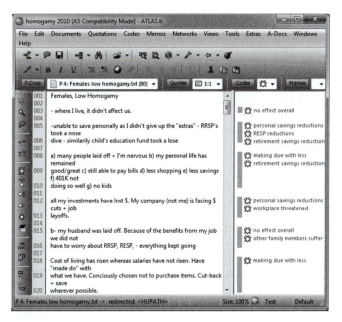

Figure 9.19   Multiple codes

Reprinted with the kind permission of ATLAS.ti Scientific Software Development GmbH.

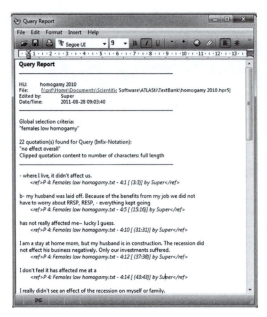

Figure 9.20 Codes and their related quotations

Reprinted with the kind permission of ATLAS.ti
Scientific Software Development GmbH.

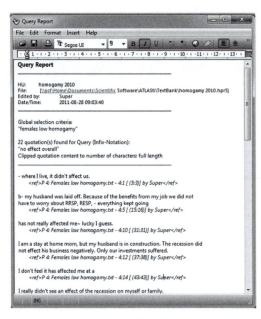

Figure 9.21 Exporting data from ATLAS.ti to
SPSS

Reprinted with the kind permission of ATLAS.ti
Scientific Software Development GmbH.

TITLE 'ATLAS.ti - homogamy 2010'.

* SPSS Syntax file generated by ATLAS.ti 6.2.27.

* SPSS Generator Version 3.2

* Date: 2011-09-16T08:16:18.

DATA LIST

FILE='\\psf\Home\Documents\ ScientificSoftware\ATLASti\SPSS\ homogamySPSS.dat' RECORDS=2

/1 CASENO (F6.0) PD (F6.0) QU (F6.0) SL (F8.0) SC (F8.0) EL (F8.0) EC (F8.0) TI (F10.0)

/2 K1 to K27 1-27.

VARIABLE LABELS PD 'Primary Doc'

/QU 'Q-Index'

/SL 'Start Line'

/SC 'Start Column'

/EL 'End Line'

/EC 'End Column'

/TI 'Creation Date'

/K1 'better off'

/K2 'bonuses reduction/lack of wage increase'

/K3 'buying power improved'

/K4 'financial difficulties other'

/K5 'general comment'

/K6 'home equity reductions'

/K7 'income reduced'

/K8 'job lost'

/K9 'job threatened'

/K10 'jobs hard to find'

/K11 'making due with less'

/K12 'no effect on income'

/K13 'no effect on job'

/K14 'no effect overall'

/K15 'opportunity for change/reflection'

/K16 'other family members okay'

/K17 'other family members suffer'

COMPUTE PF1 = 0.

IF (PD = 1 or PD = 5) PF1 = 1.

* PF2 females high homogamy.

COMPUTE PF2 = 0.

IF (PD = 6) PF2 = 1.

* PF3 females low homogamy.

COMPUTE PF3 = 0.

IF (PD = 4) PF3 = 1.

* PF4 females no rel < bach.

COMPUTE PF4 = 0.

IF (PD = 9) PF4 = 1.

* PF5 females no rel bach >.

COMPUTE PF5 = 0.

IF (PD = 10) PF5 = 1.

* PF6 males heterogamy.

COMPUTE PF6 = 0.

IF (PD = 2) PF6 = 1.

* PF7 males high homogamy.

COMPUTE PF7 = 0.

IF (PD = 3) PF7 = 1.

* PF8 males low homogamy.

COMPUTE PF8 = 0.

IF (PD = 1) PF8 = 1.

* PF9 males no rel bach >.

COMPUTE PF9 = 0.

IF (PD = 8) PF9 = 1.

* PF10 males, no rel < bach.

COMPUTE PF10 = 0.

IF (PD = 7) PF10 = 1.

FORMATS PF1, PF2, PF3, PF4, PF5, PF6, PF7, PF8, PF9, PF10 (F1).

VARIABLE LABELS PF1 'PF_females heterogamy'.

(Continued)

(Continued)

/K18 'personal savings reductions'	VARIABLE LABELS PF2 'PF_females high homogamy'.
/K19 'RESP reductions'	VARIABLE LABELS PF3 'PF_females low homogamy'.
/K20 'retirement savings reductions'	VARIABLE LABELS PF4 'PF_females no rel < bach'.
/K21 'salary reduction'	VARIABLE LABELS PF5 'PF_females no rel bach >'.
/K22 'savings grew/unaffected'	VARIABLE LABELS PF6 'PF_males heterogamy'.
/K23 'wage reductions'	VARIABLE LABELS PF7 'PF_males high homogamy'.
/K24 'work place improved'	VARIABLE LABELS PF8 'PF_males low homogamy'.
/K25 'work reductions'	VARIABLE LABELS PF9 'PF_males no rel bach >'.
/K26 'workplace steady'	VARIABLE LABELS PF10 'PF_males, no rel < bach'.
/K27 'workplace threatened'.	
	SAVE OUTFILE='homogamy 2010.sav'
VALUE LABELS K1 to K27 1 'YES' 0 'NO'.	/COMPRESSED.
* Represent primary document families as IF variables.	
* Using ALL primary document families.	
* PF1 females heterogamy.	

Figure 9.22   SPSS syntax produced in ATLAS.ti

Reprinted with the kind permission of ATLAS.ti Scientific Software Development GmbH.

Summary

In this chapter, a variety of ways to prepare for the analysis of your survey data have been presented. It is not important to grasp all of the details of analysis at this point as it takes years of practice to become fluent in the nuances of the various programs. The goal of this chapter has been to introduce you to two analytical software packages and to demonstrate how to prepare a code book in SPSS. In doing so, it is possible to test the integrity of your questionnaire and improve it before it has been administered. Also, through examples, I have demonstrated how a qualitative software program such as ATLAS.ti can be used to analyse responses to open-ended questions.

Moreover, through the use of examples, I have demonstrated that quantitative software programs are not limited to quantitative analyses, and qualitative software programs are not limited to qualitative analyses. In fact, beyond the capabilities of the individual programs, they 'talk' to each other through their 'export' and 'read' features. In other words, the programs welcome mixed methods data analysis! It is time that researchers caught up with and embraced the multifaceted features of today's data analysis tools.

Exercises

1 Locate and work through the tutorials for one quantitative software package (e.g., SPSS, SAS, Stata) and one qualitative software package (e.g., ATLAS.ti, NVivo, MAXQDA). Try R (an open source statistical analysis program).

2 Using the information in this chapter, prepare the 'code book' for your survey instrument in a quantitative software package.

3 Use text from any source and enter it into a qualitative software package. Create codes and practise coding the data. Generate lists of codes and their related quotations.

Further reading

Muhr, T., and Friese, S. (2004) *ATLAS.ti Knowledge Workbench. User's Manual and Reference.* Berlin: Scientific Software Development.
Norušis, M. (2012) *IBM SPSS Statistics 19 Advanced Statistical Procedures Companion.* Upper Saddle River, NJ: Prentice Hall.

TEN

The next steps

Having worked through the chapters of this book, you should be well prepared to conduct a survey research project. In this final chapter, I outline various ways of enhancing survey findings, discuss triangulating survey research with other methods, and augmenting findings with secondary data sources. Also, I reintroduce the topic of longitudinal and cross-sectional designs and highlight how they can be used to expand the scope of survey research. Finally, I will encourage you to think of new ways to share survey results. Many of these topics have been addressed throughout the book, but we will reconsider them through somewhat different lenses.

At this point, it is useful to revisit Chapter 2 to determine how your research project has evolved and changed through the survey design process. Has the initial research project changed, and if so, is there a need to revise the research questions so that they are in line with the current study?

TEXT BOX 10.1

Ethics Alert!

Does your original ethics application require amendment?

Through the process of designing your survey project, has your location – particularly in terms of power relations – in the study changed? If so, how? Has the intended audience for the research broadened or narrowed? Does your ethics application require amendment? Now that you have defined your sampling frame and survey instruments, what skills must you acquire to complete the analyses, and how do you intend to obtain these skills? Is your budget affordable?

What sources of funding might you pursue? Can the data be collected according to the schedule you have devised? Attention to these questions will ensure that your survey research project is sound and doable. We will now consider ways of enriching the results of your research even further.

Triangulating survey research findings

In Chapter 2, the facet 'using triangulation to determine what is already known' was introduced as a way of informing the development of your survey instrument by using existing literature to determine similarities (convergence), inconsistent and/or ambiguous claims, propositions, or results (inconsistency), and disparate approaches, theories, perspectives, analytical techniques, and results (contradiction) in the existing research. Now, this same approach can be used to further inform your well-specified survey research project. Triangulation can occur at the levels of theory, methods, and analysis.

Theoretical triangulation entails analysing your results in the light of competing or complementary theories. Do the results support one theory over another, or do they support partially one or more of the theories you have employed? If so, can you push theory development further than that of the existing literature as a result of your findings? Similarly, your results can be analysed in conjunction with analyses of existing policies, historical, and/or conceptual perspectives.

If you have embraced a mixed methods approach to your survey research project, you have already engaged in *methodological triangulation*. For example, using self-administered and interviewer-administered data collection methods allows for creative analyses of results from both perspectives. Methodological triangulation can be extended beyond survey research by adding other data collection methods such as experimental or quasi-experimental approaches, direct measurements (e.g., height and weight in the case of a health-related study on nutrition), or observations carried out in an ethnographic study. Many of the mixed methods textbooks offer designs for conducting mixed methods analyses (see, for example, Bergman, 2008a; Plano Clark and Cresswell, 2008; Tashakkori and Teddlie, 2010).

Also, *analytical triangulation* can be carried out to examine the data from multiple perspectives. Survey data are versatile in that they can be analysed in a multitude of ways in relation to research questions posed. For example, factor analysis can help to define constructs and regression analysis can be employed to determine the relationship between a dependent variable and one or more independent variables. Structural equation modelling is a sophisticated technique that combines factor analysis and regression analysis. Correspondence analysis allows for exploration of underlying data structures. Interviews can be analysed through, example, qualitative or quantitative content analysis, or through analytic induction. As we reviewed in Chapter 9, interview data can be quantified and analysed with quantitative analytical tools. The 'oomph' factor of a study, as suggested by Ziliak and McCloskey (2008), can be extended considerably through analytical triangulation.

Augmenting the findings with secondary data sources

In addition to triangulation, findings of your research project can be extended by analysing the data available in secondary data sets. Reports, such as those contained in OECD documents such as *Education at a Glance* (2010) contain data that have been prepared in the form of figures and tables. Data in this form can be used to augment your analytical arguments. Conversely, some additional analyses can be conducted using data contained in the tables. Other data sets contain raw data; that is, data are available for every individual in the sample. Examples include country-specific databases such as the British Cohort Study or the German Socio-Economic Panel Study, census and general social surveys. Also, databases with multi-country data include the World Values Survey data set and UNESCO databases. Combining small-scale studies, such as the one you are likely to conduct, with larger secondary data sets is an efficient way of maximizing the findings of your research.

Longitudinal and cross-sectional designs

Before conducting a survey research project, it is a good idea to ask yourself if it is feasible and/or desirable to consider extending the study into a longitudinal panel study or a cross-sectional study. Panel studies follow the same group of people over time. Cross-sectional studies repeat the study at different time periods with different cohorts. Often, longitudinal studies are created *ex post facto* with difficulty. In other words, having conducted a one-shot study after which the researcher or research team determined that it would be interesting to follow people over time, the researchers attempt to cobble together a follow-up. With some forethought, questions that are vital in maintaining a longitudinal study, such as contact information for the individual, can be built into the initial study. Anticipating a cross-sectional design may entail constructing survey instruments that would remain valid over time with different cohorts.

TEXT BOX 10.2

The *Scottish School-Leavers Survey* is both a longitudinal panel and cross-sectional survey research project. Do you know why this is?

http://www.esds.ac.uk/findingData/snDescription.asp?sn=5144

Sharing the results of your study

Often, research conducted in post-secondary institutions, organizations, and companies is not distributed beyond a narrow audience. Students spend several years completing master's and doctoral theses, and frequently the theses are not published in any form beyond the original formal document. Graduate students who intend to embark on academic careers may submit articles for scholarly publication, but again the audience is limited. Studies conducted within organizations such as hospitals or companies are most likely to remain in house. Unless ethics or funding arrangements do not permit dissemination, it is worth considering how your survey research project could be shared with others. By doing so, others can inform their research projects by transferring the theoretical approaches, research design, survey instruments, and results of your research.

First, if possible, your research study should be shared with the participants of your study. In Chapter 7 we reviewed the tenets of catalytic validity. Sharing the results with your participants is a step toward achieving catalytic validity in that they are invited to engage in the research project beyond the act of participating. Offering to present your findings to participants and their related communities would allow for engagement with your findings beyond the text of your project.

Another possible outlet is the media. Local, provincial or state, national, and international media organizations keep an eye on the results of interesting research. Engaging with news or popular journal media requires that you present your ideas in a straightforward way that can be easily accessible to a lay audience. Working together with a journalist may be one way of disseminating your research results to a wider audience.

When writing for an academic audience, it is critical to investigate the requirements – including topic, scope, length, research design – and style (e.g., *APA Manual, Chicago Manual of Style*) of the journal to which you plan to submit. Articles that are tailored to a given journal are much more likely to be accepted for publication. Before submitting an article, it is a good idea to request that your professors and colleagues act as 'reviewers'. By doing so, you will be provided with valuable feedback which will lead to the submission of a more polished manuscript.

Disseminating your research can also be accomplished through self-publishing. Work can be self-published in the form of blogs through to formal manuscripts. The Self-Publishing Review website (http://www.selfpublishingreview.com/) provides useful guidelines for the potential self-publisher.

Summing up

Conducting and completing a survey research project is a rewarding experience. Although there are many opportunities to make less than optimal decisions in every facet of survey research design, it is my hope that the guidance provided in this book will assist you in making informed decisions that will lead to the design of creative, strong projects with the goal of producing meaningful results. Meaningful results are those that can be translated into policies and practices with the goal of improving the lives of individuals. Hence, I conclude this book by restating the definition of survey research that I advanced in Chapter 1. The purpose of survey research is one of asking questions of the right people to elicit meaningful answers that will advance our understanding of a given topic with the goal of improving practice, policy, research, and theory.

References

American Psychological Association (2010) *Publication Manual of the American Psychological Association* (6th edition). Washington, DC: APA.

Andres, L. (2009) The cumulative impact of capital and identity construction across time: A fifteen year perspective of Canadian young women and men. In K. Robson and C. Sanders (eds), *Quantifying Theory: Bourdieu*. Berlin: Springer.

Andres, L. (2010) Education, homogamy, and inequality: A twenty-two year intergenerational perspective of Canadian women and men. Paper presented at the Society for Longitudinal and Life Course Studies Inaugural Conference, Clare College, Cambridge University, UK, 22–24 September.

Banks, J. A. (1998) The lives and values of researchers: Implications for educating citizens in a multicultural society. *Educational Researcher*, 27, 4–17.

Baron, R. M., and Kenny, D. A. (1986) The moderator-mediator variable distinction in social psychological research: Conceptual, strategic, and statistical considerations. *Journal of Personality and Social Psychology*, 51(6), 1173–1182.

Battiste, M. (2007) Research ethics for protecting indigenous knowledge and heritage: Institutional and researcher responsibilities. In N. K. Denzin and M. D. Giardina (eds), *Ethical Futures in Qualitative Research. Decolonizing the Politics of Knowledge*. Walnut Creek, CA: Left Coast Press.

Belli, R. F., Stafford, F., and Alwin, D. F. (2009) *Calendar and Time Diary: Methods in Life Course Research*. Los Angeles: Sage.

Bergman, M. M. (ed.) (2008a) *Advances in Mixed Methods Research*. London: Sage.

Bergman, M. M. (2008b) Introduction: Whither mixed methods? In M. M. Bergman (ed.), *Advances in Mixed Methods Research* (pp. 1–7). London: Sage.

Bergman, M. M. (2008c) The straw men of the qualitative-quantitative divide and their influence on mixed methods research. In M. M. Bergman (ed.), *Advances in Mixed Methods Research* (pp. 11–21). London: Sage.

Bingham, W. V. D., and Moore, B. V. (1959) *How to Interview*. New York: Harper and Brothers.

Blaxter, L., Hughes, C., and Tight, M. (2010) *How to Research* (4th edition). Maidenhead: Open University Press.

Blossfeld, H.-P. and Timm, A. (eds) (2003) *Who Marries Whom? Educational Systems as Marriage Markets in Modern Societies*. Dordrecht: Kluwer Academic.

Bollen, K. A. (1989) *Structural Equations with Latent Variables*. New York: Wiley.

Bosnjak, M., and Tuten, T. L. (2003) Prepaid and promised incentives in web surveys: An experiment. *Social Science Computer Review*, 21(2), 208–217.

Bradburn, N. M., and Sudman, S. (1979) *Improving Interview Method and Questionnaire Design*. San Francisco: Jossey-Bass.

Bradburn, N. M., and Sudman, S. (1988) *Polls and Surveys. Understanding What They Tell Us*. San Francisco: Jossey-Bass.

Bryman, A. (2008) Why do researchers integrate/combine/mesh/blend/mix/merge/ fuse quantitative and qualitative research? In M. M. Bergman (ed.), *Advances in Mixed Methods Research* (pp. 87–100). London: Sage.

Callegaro, M., and DiSogra, C. (2008) Computing response metrics for online panels. *Public Opinion Quarterly*, 72(5), 1008–1032.

Campbell, D. T., and Stanley, J. C. (1963) *Experimental and Quasi-experimental Designs for Research*. Dallas: Houghton Mifflin.

Canadian Institutes of Health Research, Natural Sciences and Engineering Research Council of Canada, and Social Sciences and Humanities Research Canada (2010) Tri-council policy statement: Ethical conduct for research involving humans, December.

Cantril, H. (1951) Foreword. In S. Payne, *The Art of Asking Questions*. Princeton, NJ: Princeton University Press.

Church, A. H. (1993) Estimating the effect of incentives on mail survey response rates: A meta-analysis. *Public Opinion Quarterly*, 57, 62–79.

Cohen, J. (1994) The earth is round ($p < .05$). *American Psychologist*, 49(12), 997–1003.

Converse, J. M. (1987) *Survey Research in the United States. Roots and Emergence 1890–1960*. Berkeley: University of California Press.

Converse, J. M., and Presser, S. (1986) *Survey Questions: Handcrafting the Standardized Questionnaire*. Thousand Oaks, CA: Sage.

Cresswell, J., Plano Clark, V. L., and Garrett, A. L. (2008) Methodological issues in conducting mixed methods research designs. In M. M. Bergman (ed.), *Advances in Mixed Methods Research* (pp. 66–83). London: Sage.

Czaja, R., and Blair, J. (2005) *Designing Surveys. A Guide to Decisions and Procedures*. Thousand Oaks, CA: Pine Forge Press.

Daston, L., and Galison, P. (2007) *Objectivity*. New York: Zone Books.

de Leeuw, E. (1992) *Data Quality in Mail, Telephone and Face to Face Surveys*. Amsterdam: TT-Publikaties.

de Leeuw, E., and Hox, J. (2008) Mixing data collection methods: Lessons from social survey research. In M. M. Bergman (ed.), *Advances in Mixed Methods Research* (pp. 138–149). London: Sage.

Denzin, N. K. (1989) *The Research Act. A Theoretical Introduction to Sociological Methods*. Englewood Cliffs, NJ: Prentice Hall.

Dillman, D. A. (2000) *Mail and Internet Surveys. The Tailored Design Method*. New York: Wiley.

Dillman, D. A., Sangster, R. L., Tarnai, J., and Rockwood, T. (1996) Understanding differences in people's answers to telephone and mail surveys. In M. T. Braverman and J. K. Slater (eds), *Advances in Survey Research Vol. 70: New Directions for Evaluation* (pp. 45–62). San Francisco: Jossey-Bass.

Edwards, J. R. (2007) Methods for integrating moderation and mediation: A general analytical framework using moderated path analysis. *Psychological Methods*, 12(1), 1–22.

Egan, G. (2010) *The Skilled Helper*. Belmont, CA: Brooks/Cole.

Englander, D., and O'Day, R. (1995) Introduction. In D. Englander and R. O'Day (eds), *Retrieved Riches* (pp. 1–46). Aldershot: Scolar Press.

Esping-Andersen, G. (1990) *The Three Worlds of Welfare Capitalism*. Princeton, NJ: Princeton University Press.

Esping-Andersen, G. (1999) *Social Foundations of Postindustrial Economies*. Oxford: Oxford University Press.

Esping-Andersen, G. (2009) *The Incomplete Revolution. Adapting to Women's New Roles*. Cambridge: Polity Press.

Fine, M., and Weis, L. (1996) Writing the 'wrongs' of fieldwork: Confronting our own research/writing dilemmas in urban ethnographies. *Qualitative Inquiry*, 2, 251–274.

Fine, M., Weis, L., Weseen, S., and Wong, L. (2000) For whom? Qualitative research, representations, and social responsibilities. In N. K. Denzin and Y. S. Lincoln (eds), *Handbook of Qualitative Research* (2nd edition). (pp. 107–131) Thousand Oaks, CA: Sage.

Fowler, F. J. J. (1995) *Improving Survey Questions*. Thousand Oaks, CA: Sage.

Fowler, F. J. J. (2009) *Survey Research Methods*. Los Angeles: Sage.

Fried, A., and Elman, R. M. (1968) *Charles Booth's London: A Portrait of the Poor at the Turn of the Century*. New York: Pantheon Books.

Galesic, M., and Bosnjak, M. (2009) Effects of questionnaire length on participation and indication of response quality in a web survey. *Public Opinion Quarterly*, 73(2), 349–360.

Garðarsdóttir, Ó., and Guðmundsson, E. G. (2005) *The Icelandic Census 1703*. Reykjavik: Statistics Iceland and National Archives of Iceland.

Grayson, P., and Myles, R. (2004) How research ethics boards are undermining survey research on Canadian university students. *Journal of Academic Ethics*, 2, 293–314.

Greene, J. C. (2007) *Mixed Methods in the Social Sciences*. San Francisco: Jossey-Bass.

Guba, E. (1981) Criteria for assessing the trustworthiness of naturalistic inquiries. *Educational Communications and Technology*, 29, 75–81.

Guppy, N., and Gray, G. (2008) *Successful Surveys: Research Methods and Practice*. Toronto: Nelson.

Henry, G. G. (1990) *Practical Sampling*. Newbury Park, CA: Sage.

Hino, A., and Imai, R. (2008) Ranking vs. rating: Re-examining the Inglehart scale through an experimental survey. Paper presented at the Panel 'Computer Assisted Self-administered Interview' at the 104th Annual Meeting of the American Political Science Association, Boston, 30 August.

Holland, J. L., and Christian, L. M. (2008) The influence of topic interest and interactive probing on responses to open-ended questions in web surveys. *Social Science Computer Review*, 27(2), 196–212.

Holmbeck, G. N. (1997) Toward terminological, conceptual, and statistical clarity in the study of mediators and moderators: Examples from the child-clinical and pediatric psychology literatures. *Journal of Consulting and Clinical Psychology*, 65(4), 599–610.

Igo, S. E. (2007) *The Averaged American: Surveys, Citizens, and the making of a Mass Public*. Cambridge, MA: Harvard University Press.

Katz, D. (1946) The interpretation of survey findings. *Journal of Social Issues*, 2(2), 33–44.

Kidder, L. (1982) Face validity from multiple perspectives. In *New Directions for Methodology of Social and Behavioral Science: Forms of Validity in Research*, no. 12 (pp. 41–57). San Francisco: Jossey-Bass.

Kirkness, V. J., and Barnhardt, R. (1991) First Nations and higher education: The four R's – respect, relevance, reciprocity, responsibility. *Journal of American Indian Education*, 30(3), 1–15.

Kish, L. (1967) *Survey Sampling*. New York: Wiley.

Krosnick, J. A. (1999) Survey research. *Annual Review of Psychology*, 50, 537–567.

Lather, P. (1986) Issues of validity in openly ideological research: Between a rock and a soft place. *Interchange*, 17(4), 63–84.

Lazarsfeld, P. (1944) The controversy over detailed interviews: An offer for negotiation. *Public Opinion Quarterly*, 8(1), 38–60.

Lazarsfeld, P. (1961) Notes on the history of quantification in sociology: Trends, sources, and problems. *Isis*, 52(2), 277–333.

Lazarsfeld, P. (1962) The sociology of empirical social research. *American Sociological Review*, 27(6), 757–767.

Lazarsfeld, P., and Oberschall, A. R. (1965) Max Weber and empirical social research. *American Sociological Review*, 30(2), 185–199.

Lincoln, Y. S., and Guba, E. (1985) *Naturalistic Inquiry.* Beverly Hills, CA: Sage.

Lynd, R. S., and Lynd, H. M. (1929) *Middletown: A Study in Contemporary American Culture.* New York: Harcourt, Brace, and Co.

Marshall, C., and Rossman, G. B. (2006) *Designing Qualitative Research.* Thousand Oaks, CA: Sage.

Mathison, S. (1988) Why triangulate? *Educational Researcher,* 17(2), 13–17.

Merriam, S. B., Johnson-Bailey, J., Lee, M.-Y., Kee, Y., Ntseane, G., and Muhamad, M. (2001) Power and positionality: Negotiating insider/outsider status within and across cultures. *International Journal of Lifelong Learning,* 20(5), 405–416.

Miles, M. B., and Huberman, A. M. (1994) *Qualitative Data Analysis: An Expanded Sourcebook.* Thousand Oaks, CA: Sage.

Muhr, T., and Friese, S. (2004) *ATLAS.ti Knowledge Workbench. User's Manual and Reference.* Berlin: Scientific Software Development.

Narayan, K. (1993) How native is a 'native' anthropologist? *American Anthropologist,* 95(3), 671–686.

Norušis, M. (2012) *IBM SPSS Statistics 19 Advanced Statistical Procedures Companion.* Upper Saddle River, NJ: Prentice Hall.

Nussbaum, M. (2002) Capabilities and social justice. *International Studies Review,* 4(2), 123–137.

OECD. (2010) *Education at a Glance.* Paris: OECD.

Onwuegbuzie, A. J. (2002) Positivists, postpositivists, post-structuralists, and post-modernists: What can't we all get along? Towards a framework for unifying research paradigms. *Education,* 122(3), 518–530.

Payne, S. (1951) *The Art of Asking Questions.* Princeton, NJ: Princeton University Press.

Pedhazur, E. J. (1982) *Multiple Regression in Behavioral Research. Explanation and Prediction.* New York: Holt, Rinehart, and Winston.

Pfautz, H. W. (1967) *Charles Booth on the City: Physical Pattern and Social Structure. Selected Writings.* Chicago: University of Chicago Press.

Plano Clark, V. L., and Cresswell, J. (2008) *The Mixed Methods Reader.* Thousand Oaks, CA: Sage.

Plowright, D. (2011) *Using Mixed Methods: Frameworks for an Integrated Methodology.* London: Sage.

Poerksen, U. (1995) *Plastic Words: The Tyranny of a Modular Language* (J. Mason and D. Cayley, trans.). University Park: Pennsylvania State University Press.

Postoaca, A. (2006) *The Anonymous Elect. Market Research through Online Access Panels.* Berlin: Springer.

Rea, L. M., and Parker, R. A. (2005) *Designing and Conducting Survey Research: A Comprehensive Guide.* San Francisco: Jossey-Bass.

Roulston, K. (2010) *Reflective Interviewing: A Guide to Theory and Practice.* Los Angeles: Sage.

Ruitenberg, C. W., and Vokey, D. (2010) Equality and justice. In R. Bailey, R. Barrow, D. Carr and C. McCarthy (eds), *The Sage Handbook of Philosophy of Education.* London: Sage.

Saris, W. E., and Gallhofer, I. N. (2007) *Design, Evaluation, and Analysis of Questionnaires for Survey Research.* Hoboken, NJ: Wiley.

Schutz, R. W., Smoll, F. L., and Gessaroli, M. E. (1983) Multivariate statistics: A self-test and guide to their utilization. *Research Quarterly,* 54(3), 255–263.

Sköld, P. (2004) The birth of population statistics in Sweden. *History of the Family,* 9, 5–21.

Smith, L. T. (1999) *Decolonizing Methodologies: Research and Indigenous Peoples.* London: Zed Books.

Stern, M. J., Dillman, D. A., and Smyth, J. D. (2007) Visual design, order effects, and respondent characteristics in a self-administered survey. *Survey Research Methods*, 1(3), 121–138.

Sudman, S. (1976) Sample surveys. *Annual Review of Sociology*, 2, 107–120.

Sudman, S., and Bradburn, N. M. (1982) *Asking Questions. A Practical Guide to Questionnaire Design*. San Francisco: Jossey-Bass.

Sue, V. M., and Ritter, L. A. (2007) *Conducting Online Surveys*. Los Angeles: Sage.

Tabachnick, B. G., and Fidell, L. S. (2006) *Using Multivariate Statistics*. New York: HarperCollins.

Tashakkori, A., and Teddlie, C. (2008) Quality of inferences in mixed methods research: Calling for an integrative framework. In M. M. Bergman (ed.), *Advances in Mixed Methods Research*. London: Sage.

Tashakkori, A., and Teddlie, C. (eds) (2010) *Handbook of Mixed Methods in social and Behavioral Research*. Thousand Oaks, CA: Sage.

Thorvaldson, G. (2007) An international perspective on Scandinavia's historical census. *Scandinavian Journal of History*, 32(3), 237–257.

Tomasson, R. F. (1977) A millennium of misery: The demography of the Icelanders. *Population Studies*, 31(3), 405–427.

Tukey, J. W. (1969) Analyzing data: Sanctification or detective work? *American Psychologist*, 33, 83–91.

Weisberg, H. F. (2005) *The Total Survey Error Approach. A Guide to the New Science of Survey Research*. Chicago: University of Chicago Press.

Yin, R. K. (1989) *Case Study Research. Design and Methods*. Newbury Park: Sage.

Ziliak, S. T., and McCloskey, D. N. (2008) *The Cult of Statistical Significance: How the Standard Error Costs Us Jobs, Justice, and Lives*. Ann Arbor: University of Michigan Press.

Index

missing values 157–158
mixed modes 45, 57
mixed methods 4, 7, 11, 22, 43, 45–46, 58, 69, 131, 169, 179, 182
moderators 41–42
    See also variables, moderators
mortality effects 127
    See also attrition

non-probabilistic samples 96–103
    See also sample, non-probabilistic

online surveys 24, 26, 45, 50–51, 77, 99, 133, 150, 170
    See also survey, online
open ended questions 47, 56, 62, 70, 158–159, 163–169
    See also questions, open ended
operationalization 33, 35
oversampling 106, 110, 127

participant 121–122
Payne, Stanley 10, 11, 15, 62, 68, 70, 72, 78, 81
pilot study 16, 27, 28, 52, 62, 65, 85, 86–87, 117, 150
    See also pre-test
plagiarism 65–66
    See also existing questions
pluralism,
    informational 20
political considerations
population 8, 92, 93
    See also target population
positionality 18–19
power dynamics 19
pre-contact information 26, 129
pre-test 27
probabilistic sampling 96, 103–109
    See also sample, probabilistic
proofreading 87
publication of results 184–185
    See also dissemination

questionnaire
    See survey
questions, ambiguous 67
    categories with multiple dimensions 78–79
    closed ended 62, 159–163, 164–167

questions, ambiguous *cont.*
    dichotomous 62, 69, 70–71, 160, 163
    double-barrelled 67, 81, 160
    existing 63–66
    fill in the blanks 77
    forced-choice 74
    instructions 68
    loaded 82
    marathon 83
    mathematical 82
    midpoints 74–75
    multiple response sets 159–162
    neutral 74–75
    no opinion 74–75
    not applicable 74–75
    on a scale of 1 to 10 75–76
    open ended 47, 56, 62, 70, 158–159, 163–169
    order 86
    ranking scales 76–77
    rating scales 72–74
    research 17, 63
    response categories 70–74
    sensitive topics 84
    series of 78
    skip instructions 86
    two way 69
    types 69–78
quotations 173–179

random sample 2, 3, 9, 97, 98, 101, 104
    See also sample, simple random
ranking scales 76–77
    See also questions, ranking scales
rating scales 72–74
    See also questions, rating scales
relationships 42
    See also variables, relationships
reliability 122–123
reminders 49, 139–140
research, assistants 129
    mixed methods 4, 7, 11, 46, 58
    mixed modes 45, 57
    problem 13, 129
    qualitative 3, 24, 46, 115, 123, 124, 127, 149
    quantitative 3, 46, 115, 149
    questions 17, 63
respondents 92, 96